PENGUIN I

AN INSIDER'S GUIDE TO
REAL ESTATE HOT SPOTS

Kieran Trass has worked in real estate for more than two decades as an investor, financier and advisor. He has spent many years specifically studying the real estate market and has developed quantitative models for enabling investors to recognise real estate opportunities. His previous book, *Grow Rich with the Property Cycle*, was published by Penguin in 2004. In 2007 Kieran will be travelling throughout the world, running seminars on real estate-related issues.

AN
INSIDER'S
GUIDE TO
REAL ESTATE
HOT SPOTS

KIERAN TRASS

PENGUIN BOOKS

PENGUIN BOOKS
Published by the Penguin Group
Penguin Group (NZ), 67 Apollo Drive, Mairangi Bay, Auckland 1310,
New Zealand (a division of Pearson New Zealand Ltd)
Penguin Group (USA) Inc., 375 Hudson Street,
New York, New York 10014, USA
Penguin Group (Canada), 90 Eglinton Avenue East, Suite 700, Toronto,
Ontario, M4P 2Y3, Canada (a division of Pearson Penguin Canada Inc.)
Penguin Books Ltd, 80 Strand, London, WC2R 0RL, England
Penguin Ireland, 25 St Stephen's Green,
Dublin 2, Ireland (a division of Penguin Books Ltd)
Penguin Group (Australia), 250 Camberwell Road, Camberwell,
Victoria 3124, Australia (a division of Pearson Australia Group Pty Ltd)
Penguin Books India Pvt Ltd, 11, Community Centre,
Panchsheel Park, New Delhi – 110 017, India
Penguin Books (South Africa) (Pty) Ltd, 24 Sturdee Avenue,
Rosebank, Johannesburg 2196, South Africa

Penguin Books Ltd, Registered Offices: 80 Strand, London, WC2R 0RL, England

First published by Penguin Group (NZ), 2006
1 3 5 7 9 10 8 6 4 2

Copyright © Kieran Trass, 2006

The right of Kieran Trass to be identified as the author of this work in terms of
section 96 of the Copyright Act 1994 is hereby asserted.

Designed by Vivianne Douglas
Typeset by Egan Reid Ltd
Prepress by Image Centre Ltd
Printed in Australia by McPherson's Printing Group

ISBN-13: 978-0-14-302100-1
ISBN-10: 0-14-302100-1
A catalogue record for this book is available
from the National Library of New Zealand.

www.penguin.co.nz

Contents

Foreword

It is said that the greatest test of will power is to refrain from saying 'I told you so!' All the same, I will indulge, as it explains why you *must* read this book.

For six straight years, I had been saying publicly, at seminars, on the radio and on television, that real estate values in Las Vegas, Nevada, had to go through the roof. This prediction of massive increases in capital values was not a random guess. It was not a premonition. It was not divine inspiration. Furthermore, I did not make hundreds of predictions in the hope that one would come true.

Rather, this prediction of Las Vegas capital values going through the roof was based purely on publicly available data, measurable facts and irrefutable realities.

To the east of Las Vegas lies Lake Mead, a large lake with a coastline of some 2200 miles formed by the Hoover Dam. To the west are the Red Rock Mountains. To the north you have Nellis

Air Force Base and American Indian Reservations. All around there is BLM land – Bureau of Land Management holdings. For land to be sold to the city of Las Vegas, the transaction has to be approved by an Act of Congress. In other words, the supply of land in Las Vegas is severely limited. The city is, in effect, 'land-locked', and there is talk of the 'Manhattenisation of Las Vegas'. Presently there is $19 billion of high-rise real estate coming out of the ground.

For years, 7000 people have been moving to Las Vegas *every month*, and only 5000 have been moving out. That means Las Vegas is growing by some 2000 residents per month. When I was making my predictions, one hundred homes a day were being built, Saturdays and Sundays included.

There are many self-appointed real estate gurus who are on the circuit peddling books, tapes and seminars, but who never do much (or any) real estate investing. Essentially, they make their money from their products. Like Kieran Trass, I am first and foremost a property investor. I put my money where my mouth is. In fact, I was so convinced about the pending spectacular growth in Las Vegas, that I set out with a former student of mine to buy *one house a week for an entire year*. We ended up acquiring the fifty-two homes in nine and a half months, and that year, 2003, capital values in Las Vegas went up *on average* by 53.7 per cent.

I emphasise 'on average', because even though Las Vegas was a hot spot in global terms, there were areas within the city that could rationally be expected to grow in value much faster than the city average. In fact, we bought a lot of our properties in the suburb of Summerlin, where growth rates that year averaged 80 per cent. Furthermore, even within the suburb of Summerlin, there were hot spots (places with great views of the Red Rock Mountains, or views of The Strip in the distance) that could reasonably be expected to grow in value much faster than the suburb average. Homes we acquired in these hot spots more than doubled that year.

I mention all of this not to boast about how smart or lucky we were, but rather to point out that it is possible to make sane, rational and calculated predictions about the emergence of real estate hot spots with a high degree of success. Unlike the investment vehicle of choice for the masses – the stock market – where the fortunes of companies and market sectors fluctuate wildly by the day and even by the hour, the fortunes of real estate markets are very slow to change. In fact, Las Vegas by most measures had held the number one position for growth in the United States for eleven years running, followed very closely by Phoenix. That's eleven *years*, not eleven hours!

Two years ago, average capital growth in Phoenix was a solid 38 per cent. Last year it was a handsome 43 per cent. This year it is likely to be somewhat less, but whatever it turns out to be, it is likely to be much higher than the national long-term average of 9.7 per cent.

Kieran Trass's *An Insider's Guide to Real Estate Hot Spots* gives you the ability to identify emerging hot spots and act rationally on hot spot data, enabling you to invest with a high likelihood of beating the average by a wide margin. There is no magic involved, no 'fiddle factor', and no information that leaves you thinking 'That can't be right!'.

Kieran strips the subject of any fluff to let you see very clearly how hot spots come about, why they can exist for a long time and, most importantly, how you can take advantage of them in your own investment decisions. Kieran is passionate about real estate and sharing his knowledge. His analysis is priceless.

By adopting the strategies that Kieran presents in *An Insider's*

Guide to Real Estate Hot Spots, you will absolutely change your odds, your wealth, and your future.

Successful Investing,

Dolf de Roos

Real Estate Investor and *New York Times* and *Wall Street Journal* best-selling author of ten books including the International Best Seller *Real Estate Riches* and *52 Homes in 52 Weeks* (both John Wiley & Sons).

Introduction

While researching and writing this book I experienced a 'paradigm' shift. I have long been a strong advocate of the 'buy and hold' real estate investment strategy. This strategy is exactly what it says . . . buy and hold, that's it. Buy a property, rent it out and keep it long-term. Don't get me wrong, I am still an advocate of the 'buy and hold' strategy. It is a great way to grow rich and accumulate large amounts of wealth over time, and that's the key word here – time. It takes time for real estate values to rise. Of course, if you are lucky or informed enough to recognise what's driving demand, you can buy into a location just before it booms.

The 'buy and hold' strategy has a lot going for it: it is usually a relatively slow, but very safe, way to build wealth. Using this strategy I have enjoyed the cyclical capital growth real estate ownership delivers. However, on occasions I have been disappointed when some of the suburbs, neighbouring those I owned investment real estate in, suddenly shot up in value while my investment real estate was not increasing in value at all. Where was my capital growth? Why did my real estate value not increase by 20 per cent in a year too? I did have some success investing in locations that surged in value pretty much as soon as I bought in them, but in my early days of investing it was sheer luck, not by design.

I used to be resigned to the fact that the more expensive locations must get superior capital growth because they always seemed to be getting more expensive in relation to properties in cheaper suburbs. My perception was that better locations enjoyed better capital growth. It wasn't until I studied historic capital growth rates that I found this not to be the case at all. In fact, there were periods when the cheapest locations in a town/city/ country experienced far superior growth rates than the most expensive locations. It became obvious that hot spots can emerge anywhere and so my quest to find out why they had emerged began in earnest.

It soon became apparent that certain changes within any location can markedly increase its desirability, subsequent demand for occupants and, therefore, values. When I considered what had caused these changes I found some pretty common reasons. My findings are within this book.

The many locations I considered in my research were different from each other in numerous ways, some had features which command a price premium, like sea views, while others were the cheapest locations in town. Interestingly, some of the cheaper locations had shown periods of achieving more capital growth than some of the best parts of the same town! So my assumption that the best locations get the highest capital growth was incorrect. It also became apparent that there was a cyclical pattern of capital growth which impacted on certain parts of town, creating what I term 'cyclical hot spots'. Hot spots will always emerge when there is a rapid increase in demand to occupy dwellings, but the discovery of relatively predictable 'cyclical hot spots' brought a new dimension of risk minimisation to my real estate investing.

The concept of real estate hot spots is not new, but the study of how to identify them seems to be a relatively uncharted territory.

This book will teach you the basic principles of how to identify real estate hot spots and how you can use them to accumulate or protect your real estate wealth.

Learning this knowledge and applying it can be likened to having a real estate gold pan.

Unfortunately, this will not make you immune from finding fool's gold, but hopefully it will better equip you to know the difference between fool's gold and real gold.

Identifying real estate hot spots before they emerge is not simple or assured, but if you treat such a quest seriously and make the effort to surround yourself with better-quality information you can make better-quality decisions.

Capital growth in any location is typically erratic and not uniformly predictable.

However, if you understand how the combination of certain impacting factors can influence the demand for real estate, then you can learn how hot spots may emerge.

If you intend to speculate by investing in real estate hot spots then caveat emptor or 'buyer beware' still applies. The old adage: 'You make your money when you buy', also applies to buying in real estate hot spots.

Ironically, identifying real estate hot spots is not all about Location, Location, Location – it's about Research, Research, Research.

Be wary of hearsay about where the next hot spot may be as it will only be a few people's opinion and is often outdated by the time you hear it. Worse still, by the time the message gets to you the suburb may have been confused with another suburb or the facts distorted. *Never* guess – do your homework!

Be aware that history is your friend but doesn't always repeat *exactly*. You need to research plenty of information and get a feel for the market, and you also need to understand the buyer market that will pay you your profit when you eventually sell the real estate.

The main purpose of this book is to provide you with the background of my research into real estate hot spots. It also contains some tools to increase your chances of getting your timing right. *An Insider's Guide to Real Estate Hot Spots* also provides a starting framework within which you can measure the 'Hot Spot Drivers' for any location to ascertain whether it currently is, or will soon become, a real estate hot spot. I would encourage you to 'test' the systems in this book by measuring the hot spot drivers in locations in your own town, city or country, before you choose to use them to help your real estate investment decision-making. Your feedback is welcome and encouraged, and it supports my further research. I don't profess to have all of the answers about real estate hot spots and I am always open to learning from the experience of others. Experience is sometimes the best teacher, so if you can combine your experience with mine then we can both get a better understanding of this topic. Please don't think twice about giving me your feedback at: kieran@tellmethetime.com

While I personally have had a good level of success investing in real estate hot spots, the results of the research I have undertaken have opened up a new style of investing for me and I hope they do for you too. The study has provided fresh insights into a whole new spectrum of real estate and equipped me to make safer, and therefore better, decisions. It's true that I have no formal qualifications so my analysis has a very limited degree of widely recognised analytical technique, if any.

Of course, you don't have to act on any of the information you read in this book and if you do act on it, and try investing in a real estate hot spot, then there is some level of risk attached. Personally I have never lost money on any real estate investments, but that doesn't mean I will never lose, so I have devised my own 'stop loss' system to try to minimise that risk. Using the principles and systems in this book as my guide, and with a calculated level of risk, I'm personally planning to embark on an international journey to invest in real estate hot spots around the globe. This book, therefore, is considered a starting point and not my final words on the topic. I hope it can be your guide too. If nothing else, I trust this book gives you the opportunity to minimise your real estate investing risks.

Acknowledgements

My major inspiration has been my business partner, the love of my life and wife, Jo. You have often given me strength when I have needed it most. When the going gets tough I know you are always there.

David and Gaylene, thanks for access to 'the beach hut', where I have been able to write in peace and quiet without distractions. It has clearly been an inspiration!

1

What Defines a Real Estate Hot Spot?

- ▶ What is a real estate hot spot?
- ▶ The different types of real estate hot spots
- ▶ What is the ripple effect?
- ▶ The predictability of the ripple effect
- ▶ The impact of time on risk
- ▶ The levels of potential risk and potential return

What is a real estate hot spot?

The common perception seems to be that a real estate hot spot is a suburb or location that experiences strong capital growth. But does that mean a hot spot is a suburb or location that has *already had* strong capital growth or is it a suburb or location that is *about to have* strong capital growth?

There are five *types* of real estate hot spots, which are explained in the next few pages, showing real estate hot spots can either be about to have strong capital growth (i.e. a *likely* or *emerging* hot spot) or have already had recent strong capital growth (i.e. an *existing* hot spot).

So, does that mean that just because an existing hot spot is experiencing strong capital growth, it will continue to be a real estate hot spot? Equally, how will you know whether a suburb or location is about to become a hot spot when it is yet to demonstrate any strong capital growth?

This book answers these questions by providing an insight into why real estate hot spots emerge and how you can identify them.

Definition of a real estate hot spot

A real estate hot spot is a location that is experiencing or about to experience rapid, strong and sustainable capital growth.

The main elements of real estate hot spots, in respect of capital growth, are as follows:

1. **Rapid** capital growth – either experiencing or about to experience *rapid* capital growth (rapid = within a three-month period)

2. **Strong** capital growth – such capital growth must be *strong* (strong = more than 4 per cent for a single quarter)

3. **Sustainable** capital growth – such capital growth must be *sustainable* (sustainable = real estate values do not fall back to the level they were at prior to such rapid and strong growth).

A real estate hot spot must demonstrate *all three* of these elements because:

1. Rapid and strong growth alone may not prove sustainable
2. Rapid and sustainable growth alone may not prove strong
3. Strong and sustainable growth alone may not prove rapid.

The phrase 'real estate hot spot' conjures up powerfully emotive visions of real estate values doubling in just a few months or years, resulting in huge amounts of money being made from correctly timing the buying and then subsequent selling of real estate.

If you get your timing right, you can create significant wealth and multiply your initial investment, especially if you achieve leverage through borrowing funds to assist with the purchase of the property. If you get your timing wrong, however, the impact can multiply your losses and destroy significant wealth too!

Using some of the principles and systems in this book, in 2001 I commenced a journey to multiply my wealth by investing in real estate hot spots. Traditionally I have pursued the 'buy and hold' real estate investing strategy, which has proven to be a sure and steady way to successfully create wealth from real estate.

In 2001 I decided to test my limited knowledge (at that time) of hot spots. I decided to earmark $20,000 to invest in just one property that I intended to hold long term, but which I would try to buy in a hot spot location that would achieve strong capital growth immediately after I had bought there. Then I intended to borrow against the increased value of that property to use as a deposit on more property in more hot spots, and then repeat that pattern as often as I needed to so I could achieve a very high return on my initial investment. This wasn't about blindly guessing where to buy; I needed to do as much research as I could *before* I bought so that I could maximise my potential return and minimise my financial risk at the same time.

I decided to use a relatively passive strategy of buying real estate to retain long term, but to still make sure I achieved strong capital growth in the first year of ownership. Using this very strategy I turned my original $20,000 into more than $600,000 in equity from just a few real estate transactions, all with a calculated level of risk and within just four years.

Recently I have been referred to as a real estate 'money magician' because of my ability to generate wealth from investing in real estate, but I'm not. I have just observed and identified patterns that affect real estate values, and then formulated ways to measure those patterns and assess the likelihood of surges in real estate values as a result. The more than $580,000 wealth I created was a staggering compounding return for four years of more than 130 per cent per annum on my initial $20,000 investment. Because I was aware the real estate cycle was about to enter a boom in 2002, I focused on seeking out locations that would outperform the capital growth rates of other locations in the same city and deliver at least 20 per cent capital growth in the first year of ownership. My initial strategy was, therefore, to invest in what I now deem 'cyclical' hot spots (cyclical hot spots are discussed later in this chapter).

Typical real estate hot spots are likely to emerge due to a major improvement in the desirability of a location. Such an improvement in desirability is usually due to a combination of factors, which all contribute at the same time to increased demand. I call these factors, which can collectively create the perfect environment for a hot spot to emerge, 'hot spot drivers'. (See Chapter 3 for more detail.)

The best-performing hot spots will have many hot spot drivers, collectively responsible for creating a substantial positive shift in the perception of the desirability of the location.

When you learn to recognise the hot spot drivers that indicate a hot spot will emerge, you can relatively easily capitalise on short-term capital growth.

Often people don't understand why hot spots emerge in the first place so they simply buy real estate in a location they perceive to be a real estate hot spot only to be disappointed by little or no capital growth in the ensuing months or even years. Sometimes it's even worse than that and values decline.

Hot spots can emerge at any time but tend to be more prevalent during the recovery and boom phases of the real estate cycle (see Chapter 8). In particular this is when 'cyclical' hot spots emerge. This does not mean that hot spots cannot emerge during a real estate slump, because when adequate hot spot drivers influence a location, it will become a hot spot irrespective of the real estate cycle's phase at that time.

There is sometimes a general perception that real estate values will increase simply because they *must* be due for strong growth. Typically this perception emerges when a suburb or location has had negative, no, or little capital growth for a long period of time. Investing in real estate based on a general perception that values will increase is a high-risk strategy that I do not recommend.

On the other hand, sometimes hot spots are overlooked by real estate investors who are too focused on buying in the cheapest suburbs or locations of town to recognise that hot spots can emerge in superior suburbs or locations too.

Once a suburb or location is widely known as a hot spot then that location has most likely already had the large majority of its capital growth.

Be aware that there are also contradictions to hot spot drivers (refer to Chapter 3 for more information).

The different types of real estate hot spots

There are five different types of real estate hot spots to bear in mind.

It is important to identify the various types of hot spots because they have varying degrees of risk or the potential for loss, and varying degrees of potential return. Some types of hot spots have specific hot spot drivers which can be used to identify which type of hot spot they are.

Below I have identified the different types of hot spots that can exist and estimated a level of potential return and potential loss for each.

Traditional hot spots follow a typical progression from being a possible hot spot, which demonstrates some early signs of hot spot drivers, through to an existing hot spot, which is a location demonstrating many hot spot drivers in action.

Types of hot spots

Traditional

Possible – A location which demonstrates *early signs* that hot spot drivers are emerging or likely to emerge.

Likely – A location which clearly demonstrates *some* hot spot drivers have emerged.

Emerging – A location which demonstrates *many* hot spot drivers in action combined with already having achieved *strong capital growth in the last three months.*

Existing – A location which demonstrates *many* hot spot drivers in action combined with already having achieved *strong capital growth in the last six months.*

Non-traditional

Cyclical – A location which demonstrates *strong capital growth cyclically* at a consistent phase in the real estate cycle.

Hot spots will typically progress through these different types as follows:

Possible	→	Likely	→	Emerging	→	Existing

Locations become possible hot spots when they demonstrate some early signs that hot spot drivers exist. When those drivers emerge the location becomes a likely hot spot and then when there are many drivers it becomes an emerging hot spot. When consistent strong growth rates are achieved it becomes an existing hot spot.

Any hot spot can also quickly become a *stop* spot (i.e. no growth), and sometimes a hot spot will cease to be altogether in a very short period of time. The timeframe before it ceases being a hot spot will be determined by the combination of hot spot drivers impacting on the location.

Cyclical hot spots

Cyclical hot spots occur as a result of the real estate cycle's progress. They don't tend to follow the progress of traditional hot spots and can occur seemingly unannounced, particularly if you are not observing the real estate cycle's progress. Cyclical hot spots will, however, emerge at a consistent phase in the real estate cycle, which makes them relatively predictable.

Cyclical hot spots appear during the recovery and boom phases of every real estate cycle. They typically occur when a location suddenly experiences a surge in rents and value growth rates subsequently rapidly rise – this traditionally occurs in the superior neighbourhoods of a city. When rents increase in these initial cyclical hot spots some tenants will be unable to afford the increased rents and so will be forced to move out of these desirable suburbs and into more affordable mid-socio-economic locations.

Often they will move into slightly cheaper but neighbouring suburbs to the high socio-economic locations. This in turn places more pressure on rents in the mid-socio-economic locations. As this pattern repeats it creates a ripple effect on both rents and values.

Cyclical Hot Spots Secrets

Study the past to see the pathway to the future. If certain areas within a city are found to always lead to capital growth early in the cycle then you should direct your investment to the most appropriate area at the most appropriate point in the real estate cycle.

What is the ripple effect?

The ripple effect is the term used when values surge in a suburb and then the same occurs in a neighbouring suburb (usually within a few months of the initial suburb's value surge) and then the same occurs in a neighbouring suburb of the second suburb and so on, creating a ripple effect of increasing values, moving from one suburb to the next. The ripple effect commences because of cyclical hot spots emerging in the recovery and boom phases of the real estate cycle as explained above.

The pattern the ripple effect follows is similar to the ripple created from throwing a pebble into a still pond.

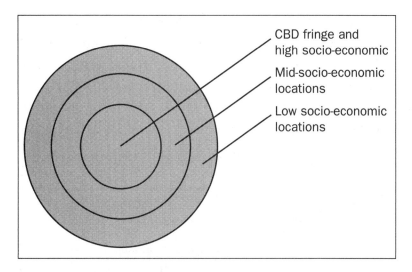

CBD fringe and
high socio-economic

Mid-socio-economic
locations

Low socio-economic
locations

Figure 1.1

The ripple effect typically begins in the high socio-economic locations in a central business district fringe and/or the best locations nearest to the 'heart' of a city.

During the real estate cycle recovery and early to mid-boom phases generally, value growth patterns follow the trend of emanating from near the centre of a city and then circling out (but not precisely) across the rest of the city, which is why values in a location on the outskirts of a city can be rising while values in the better parts of the city are experiencing lower rates of capital growth.

The predictability of the ripple effect

The ripple effect is relatively predictable, although not as precise as illustrated below.

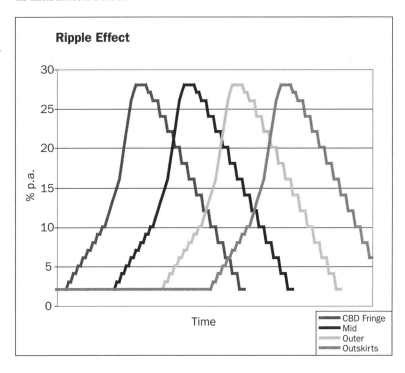

Graph 1.1

Ripple Effect Secrets

Buy early in the ripple in the best locations you can afford. Then buy in the next best suburbs typically on the neighbouring parts of the city fringe.

The impact of time on risk

It is important to take into consideration the impact of time on investing in real estate because time increases risk.

There is a correlation between time and risk when you invest in real estate because there are ongoing 'holding costs'. I describe holding costs as any shortfall between income (rents) and total ownership expenses as a result of owning the real estate. Holding costs can be as high as 10 per cent per annum (or even more) of your total investment. So, as time passes and your total investment increases, so too do your holding costs and thus your risk. The larger your total investment, the more you have at risk and the higher the opportunity cost because of the time elapsed.

I have devised a basic measure to illustrate the impact of time on risk as follows:

r = risk

t = time expired (i.e. quarters or three-month periods)

hc = holding costs for a quarter (estimated at $2,500 per quarter for this example)

So, for the purpose of this illustration, risk = time expired – holding costs ÷ 1000 (i.e. $2,500 ÷ 1000 = 2.5$)

$r = t - (hc \div 1000)$

$1 = 1 - 2.5 = -1.5$	$6 = 6 - 2.5 = 3.5$
$2 = 2 - 2.5 = -0.5$	$7 = 7 - 2.5 = 4.5$
$3 = 3 - 2.5 = 0.5$	$8 = 8 - 2.5 = 5.5$
$4 = 4 - 2.5 = 1.5$	$9 = 9 - 2.5 = 6.5$
$5 = 5 - 2.5 = 2.5$	$10 = 10 - 2.5 = 7.5$

Below is the graph showing my measure of risk associated with buying in a hot spot.

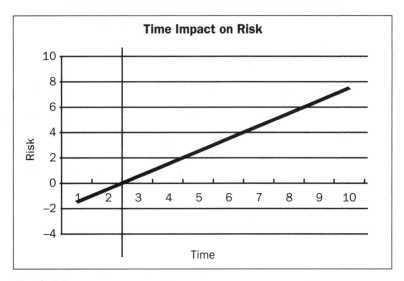

Graph 1.2

On the risk scale (refer to Graph 1.2):

▶ The lower the number the lower the risk

▶ The shorter the ownership timeframe the lower the risk

▶ For each quarter of ownership the level of risk increases.

My estimate, based on the above graph, implies that to *minimise risk* ideally a location needs to emerge as a hot spot within *two to three quarters* (i.e. six to nine months) of buying property there.

Time management is the issue here. You need to manage the length of time you own the property. Your ownership should be for less than nine months, preferably six months, to keep your risk to a minimum. This is why it becomes critical to learn how you can increase your odds of buying in a hot spot. Time will be your biggest enemy unless it delivers strong capital growth and quickly.

The levels of potential risk and potential return

It is important with any investment to assess the potential return against the potential risk in terms of a potential loss associated with that return. So I have considered each type of hot spot to assess the type with the highest potential return but the lowest risk.

When I considered what may impact on risk, I found that time was a big factor financially either in cost or lost opportunity. Financial cost occurs because of ownership costs and lost opportunity because if you hadn't bought the property you could have earned interest on the cash instead. The more time expires, the more risk therefore exists.

Bear in mind that the level of potential return can be high for most types of hot spots, especially if you apply leverage by borrowing to increase your exposure to real estate instead of just paying the purchase price in cash.

The graph on the following page gives an indication of the various levels of risk and return for each type of hot spot. As a traditional hot spot progresses through its various stages the level of potential return reduces until it becomes an existing hot spot. The greatest potential loss exists in possible hot spots and reduces as the hot spot progresses through its various stages. The risk is at its lowest for an emerging hot spot before it increases again once it becomes an existing hot spot.

Cyclical hot spots are my favourite as they offer a relatively high potential return but the lowest level of potential loss.

Possible – Obviously if you buy early before a location has rapid and strong growth then you can maximise your return, but your risk is also higher as the location may not emerge as a hot spot for many years.

Likely – A likely hot spot can also deliver a strong return but

31

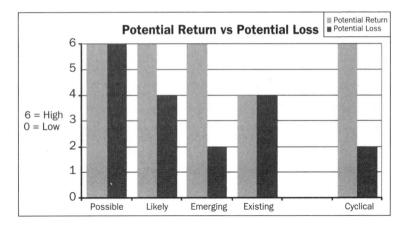

Graph 1.3

could still take too long to emerge. A likely hot spot is already demonstrating some hot spot drivers. So a likely hot spot has a slightly lower level of risk than a possible hot spot.

Emerging – An emerging hot spot is already emerging so has a potentially lower return than a likely hot spot. It also has an even lower level of risk because an emerging hot spot has already achieved strong capital growth in the last three months.

Existing – An existing hot spot has the lowest potential return and a higher level of risk than an emerging hot spot, because an existing hot spot has already emerged and had strong capital growth in the last six months. The potential return is still reasonable even though you have missed the strong initial growth rates, but the potential for loss is increased because the location may quickly cease to be a hot spot at any point in time when supply exceeds demand.

Cyclical – Cyclical hot spots have the lowest risk for the best potential return. They can provide great opportunity with little risk, but only if you have good insights into the concepts of the real estate cycle (Chapter 8) and the ripple effect.

Based on this assessment the safest types of hot spots to invest in appear to be emerging and cyclical hot spots because they offer potentially lower risk. In comparison, possible hot spots appear the most risky because while they still offer a potentially high return they also bring the highest degree of risk.

Below is an indication of which types of hot spots are likely to suit you depending on how aggressive or passive you plan to be by investing in hot spots (refer to Chapter 5 for further details on aggressive and passive goals).

Conservative: Emerging, cyclical

Neutral: Existing

Aggressive: Possible, likely.

Chapter Summary

▶ A real estate hot spot is a location that is experiencing or about to experience rapid, strong and sustainable capital growth.

▶ Hot spots can emerge at any time but regularly emerge during very buoyant times in the real estate cycle, sometimes even in a cyclical pattern.

▶ Sometimes hot spots are overlooked by real estate investors who are too focused on buying in the cheapest suburbs or locations in town to recognise that hot spots can emerge in superior suburbs or locations too.

▶ There are five different types of real estate hot spots: traditional hot spots are either possible, likely, emerging or existing and progress from one to the next. Cyclical hot spots do not follow the traditional pattern of emergence.

▶ To minimise risk a location needs to become a hot spot within two to three quarters (i.e. six to nine months) of buying property there.

▶ It is important to identify the various types of hot spots because they have varying degrees of risk or the potential for loss, and varying degrees of potential return.

▶ The ripple effect typically commences on the back of the real estate cycle entering the recovery phase.

▶ High socio-economic locations in a central business district fringe and/or the best locations nearest to the heart of a city are usually the first to experience the ripple effect.

▶ It is important to take into consideration the time impact on investing in real estate because time increases risk.

▶ The safest types of hot spots to invest in appear to be emerging and cyclical hot spots because they offer potentially lower risk but a potentially high return.

2

CHAPTER

Hot Spot, or Not?

▶ Are you flying by sight only?
▶ Why you need 'special dials'
▶ Misleading or flawed data
▶ How to spot self-interested media releases

Are you flying by sight only?

Successful investment in real estate requires access to quality information; this is critical to help minimise your risks. If you don't use reliable information, you can easily end up buying real estate in a location you think may be a hot spot, but in fact it's not.

It was while seeking to define what real estate market information is needed to identify hot spots that I realised much of the information available had limited value due to its poor quality. Frequently, the information was potentially unreliable and certainly not suitable as the basis for large financial decisions, such as purchasing real estate.

A good example of this is the common use of median or average real estate price data when making real estate purchasing decisions. (I outline the details of the inaccuracy of this data later in this chapter.)

I found that much information available, particularly relating to capital growth rates within specific suburbs in a city, was sub-standard and could therefore easily lead to poor real estate investment decisions as a result.

In this chapter I have outlined the quality of information and the technical instruments, or 'special dials', as I call them, which I now rely on to make safer real estate investment decisions.

It was as a passenger on an aeroplane that the true value of using technical instruments to minimise risks became apparent to me. No, this isn't a story of a mid-air crisis but more of a mid-air realisation.

I was sitting next to a young boy (accompanied by his mother) on the aeroplane and as we were approaching to land he asked, 'Are we flying through a cloud?' Looking out the window I saw that we were flying through a cloud so I replied, 'Yes'. Then he asked, 'So how can the pilots see where we are going?' Amused at his question, but understanding it was a very sensible one for a young boy to ask, I explained that pilots have some 'special dials' that they can read to tell them where the plane is and where it is going, even when they can't *see* where it is going. I explained that this is also how they can safely fly the plane at night when it's very dark and they can't see out the windows.

His reply to that surprised me when he asked suspiciously, 'So why do the pilots have windows at all then?' I was again very amused by his question but understood the logic behind his suspicion. Of course, his question made perfect sense, because if pilots could just read their 'special dials' they wouldn't ever need to see outside so why would they need windows at all? After I again got over my initial amusement at his question, I explained that it is important for pilots to be able to see where they are going by looking out the windows, but when they can't see outside, because of cloud or night-time, they have their 'special dials' to fly the plane.

He then seemed to understand the value of having both dials to gauge where the plane is when the pilots can't see out the windows and having windows for a means of sight when they can.

This conversation got me thinking about how appropriate the concept of using both 'sight' and 'special dials' is to maximising wealth creation through real estate.

My mid-air realisation was that when I first began my quest for real estate wealth in the late 1980s I originally relied purely on my sight to make decisions on which location to buy real estate in and when to buy. My sight was simplistic but it was all I knew at the time. I was unaware that my sight was giving me a 'clouded' view, and it took me over a decade to realise it.

Like all those seeking to profit from owning real estate I had to make some decisions. Decisions like *when* and *where* I should buy, *how much* I would spend and *what type* of property I should buy.

To decide *when* to buy I simply waited until I qualified for enough funding to be able to buy a property, and ascertaining *how much* I would spend was determined by how much the bank would lend me. To ascertain *where* I would buy I decided to simply buy in or near the suburb I had grown up in, and *what type* of property I would buy was fixed early on: it had to have two bedrooms that I could easily transform into three bedrooms so I could increase the property value.

That was the extent of my 'sight' in helping me make decisions when first deciding to invest in real estate.

In 1987 I finally qualified for a mortgage so that answered my question of *when* to buy and also *how much* I could spend. Deciding *where* I could buy was easy too, because I quickly found the *type* of property I wanted for sale in a suburb close to where I had grown up.

The problem was that my sight was being clouded. Clouded because I was unaware that the location I was about to purchase my first property in was soon to suffer a significant (20 per cent) decrease in real estate values (within just eighteen months of my purchase). My clouded sight told me real estate values always increased (simply because they had appeared to historically over a long period of time).

My method of using sight alone was extremely limited and was so clouded that I really couldn't see much at all even though I was convinced I could see what the real estate market was doing at the time. I mistakenly thought real estate values would continue to rise in the next few years because they had in the past, but they didn't . . . until many years later. The only redeeming feature of this first property purchase was that I had the extra bedroom built in the partially developed basement therefore transforming the property from a two-bedroom into a three-bedroom property. The effect of adding the extra room was that it fortunately increased the value of the property so much that I made a 20 per cent profit when I sold it eighteen months later.

When it came to my second property purchase I thought I had learned a lot from my first experience and knew I needed better information to make a better purchasing decision. So I decided to do more research to enhance my sight, in particular to help me decide where to buy.

The research I undertook this time included:

▶ Considering recent median real estate price growth in the location I grew up in and in the surrounding suburbs
▶ Finding out how much other properties had sold for in those locations over the previous twelve months.

I found out that a suburb right next to the suburb I had grown up in had performed better than the surrounding suburbs over the last few years based on the movement of median real estate prices, so I decided to buy there. My theory was that if this suburb had superior growth in the last few years then it would probably continue to do so in the next few. I was unaware of how misleading median prices can be on a localised suburb basis.

Finding out how much properties had been selling for was fairly simple as real estate agents/realtors were only too happy to tell me about 'comparable' sales they had made in the location. I was unaware that the real estate agents I was discussing my purchasing needs with had a vested interest in only telling me about the properties which had sold for relatively high prices in the location.

This research did, however, make me feel much more confident in deciding where to buy and how much I should pay for my next property.

The research may have made me feel better but, unbeknown

to me at the time, this second property purchase was not so good either. I was still using sight only. I purchased a two-bedroom house in the suburb, nearly two years after my first property purchase. Again I simply bought near where I had grown up and again my timing was based on my ability to raise adequate mortgage finance to complete the purchase. This time, in the three years following my purchase, the suburb decreased significantly in value. Combine this with the fact that I paid more than the property was probably worth at the time of my purchase, and the scene was set to potentially end in my bankruptcy! If instead I had bought in a different location within the same city, I could have achieved some capital growth, as some suburbs did not fall in value during this time.

The redeeming feature of this second property purchase was exactly the same as my first: as soon as I bought it I had an extra bedroom built in the partially developed basement, therefore transforming the property into a three-bedroom property. This had proved my winning formula previously, so surely it would work again. Unfortunately, my winning formula failed because even the effect of adding the extra bedroom was not enough to stop the value of this property falling by more than 25 per cent over the following three years.

Worse still, I didn't even use any 'sight' method to decide when to sell any property; instead I would sell if I needed a lump of cash. For example, when I started my first business in 1996 I sold a property to fund my start-up business irrespective of the real estate market. That property increased in value over the next year by around 21 per cent because it was located in a real estate hot spot at the time, but I didn't know that then.

If I had understood then how to identify real estate hot spots, I would certainly have delayed the sale for another year and borrowed against the property to start my business instead of selling the property.

You may be thinking I'm a slow learner because it wasn't until I had been investing for over a decade before I recognised the need to have some technical instruments to help make safer real estate investment decisions. Experience taught me that often my view of the real estate market could easily be distorted or misrepresented. I needed better tools to make better decisions – I needed some 'special dials'. The problem I found was that there were few, if any, effective tools or 'special dials' available to help pinpoint suitable locations to buy in or to calculate the right timing to buy or sell real estate.

Relying purely on your own perception of how things look, without obtaining quality information, can be devastating. Just imagine you are a pilot flying an aeroplane without any 'special dials' so you have to rely on your sight only. You are approaching the airport and think you can see the runway you intend to land on but your view is partially blocked by clouds. It is not until you get closer and are already committed to landing that you realise you are off course: it's not the runway at all, just a strip of land that through the clouds had looked like the runway!

Pilots have 'special dials' to minimise their risks and the same principle applies to investing in real estate. If you have no 'special dials' then you have a substantially increased level of risk. You cannot rely on sight alone as it may be distorted or be giving you a deceptive view. This is how you can easily lose money or, worse still, get financially wiped out by real estate investment.

In 2000, I came to the conclusion that I needed more than just my own visual perception of the real estate market to safely make wise decisions about investing millions more dollars in real estate. It wasn't that I had lost any money through real estate investment, because I hadn't. Even though the values of my first few purchases actually fell shortly after I bought them, I retained ownership of them for many years until their values had substantially increased. But I knew there must be a better way to invest than that!

So, in 2000, I set out on a quest to find out what the most useful 'special dials' may be to help make more money from real estate investing with less risk. I already knew from much experience what a 'good real estate deal' looked like, so this wasn't a quest to increase my knowledge base about smarter real estate investing, far from it in fact. I knew what *type* of properties I wanted to buy and I no longer determined *how much* I could spend based on the maximum amount I could afford to borrow.

This was more of a quest to better understand the real estate market. I needed some special dials to help me read the real estate market better and answer a few key questions which seemed to have ever-changing answers.

My key questions revolved around not what *type* of real estate or *how much* I should spend, but instead *when* and *where* to buy or sell as I had gotten my timing and locations so wrong in my early days of investing. I already understood it was always the right time to buy *if* you buy right (i.e. at a significant discount), but my need was to understand more about timing and location.

My three key questions were:

How will I know *when* it is a good time to buy?
How will I know *when* it is a good time to sell?
How can I decide *where* I should buy to benefit from strong capital growth in the short term?

I sought answers to my questions but frankly was disappointed with the plethora of biased opinion on when and where I should buy and why. Many of the answers came from those within the real estate industry who had vested interests in promoting 'now' as always a good time to buy in the specific location they happened to be selling real estate in. It seems that many in the real estate industry are convinced that their local real estate market is a hot spot waiting to be found or in some cases they promote their location as being a permanent hot spot. Permanent hot spots are a fallacy, they do not exist. No location can have permanent and strongly increasing real estate values of 20 per cent per annum forever.

Disillusioned with the lack of genuinely unbiased answers to my questions I realised that I had little choice but to set about creating my own 'special dials'. So again I started with my key questions.

To answer these questions I first had to investigate whether the 'big picture' of the real estate market could be considered within some sort of framework that revolved around timing. From my years of observation of real estate price movements combined with observing the 'big picture' of the real estate market while working within the finance industry for twenty years, I had enough evidence to prove it certainly was cyclical to some degree. The 'big picture' I considered was the fact that, geographically, real estate locations appeared to respond collectively to a certain extent. For example, when suburbs within a city had strong real estate value appreciation (capital growth) then eventually every suburb of that city had some capital growth. Some suburbs did overachieve compared to others, but generally the whole city's real estate values benefited. So my initial research focused on the concept of the real estate cycle, whether it actually existed at all and if so whether it could be fairly accurately predicted or not. The culmination of that specific research was my book *Grow Rich with the Property Cycle.* In that book I reached the conclusion that not only does the real estate cycle exist in any country's residential real estate market (where supply and demand are driven by a free market), but that it is measurable and even quite predictable!

Once I understood the concept of the traditional real estate cycle I realised that it provided part of the answer to my timing questions.

So I decided I needed to use a suitable image to 'track' the progress of the real estate cycle, an image to use as a tool to measure where a real estate market is, at any point in time, in relation to the real estate cycle. Therefore my first 'dial' was created and I call it the real estate cycle clock. (In Chapter 8, I outline the intricacies of this concept in detail.)

Since creating the real estate cycle clock in 2001, I have been tracking the progress of the real estate cycle in many countries, such as the USA, UK, Australia and New Zealand. In New Zealand I have also been using it to accurately predict the cycle's progress since 2001. This dial has proved invaluable in enabling me to recognise that the New Zealand real estate boom of 2002–06 was coming *before* it arrived. This gave me the ability to purchase real estate in 2001 to capitalise on the coming boom just before it arrived. In hindsight it now may appear obvious that a real estate boom was coming, but in 2001 very few people believed it.

So the real estate cycle clock has proved a useful dial for me to understand and measure the progress of the real estate cycle. While useful from the 'big picture' timing perspective, for example, to measure where a country or city may be in relation to the real estate cycle, it didn't, however, give me any clues to which suburb or location in a city I should buy within. While it provided me with part of the answer to my timing questions, it was not very useful in helping me decide where to buy.

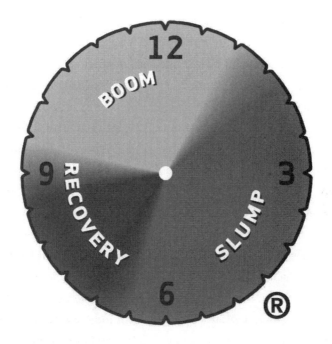

Real Estate Cycle Clock

That's when I realised that I still needed some way to measure where to buy to benefit from strong capital growth in the short term. It wasn't that I necessarily wanted to buy and then sell every property for pure speculation, but it was about minimising my risk of loss and not repeating the timing mistakes I had made on my first few property purchases.

So, now I had one dial but I knew I needed another. I started researching the history of real estate price movements in the city I had traditionally invested in. The facts I compiled were limiting, to say the least. I was already wise to the fact that median data was misleading so I sought a better-quality house price measure.

I found that many economists relied on a House Price Index (HPI) measure to monitor the movements of real estate values. The HPI was not prone to the distortions that median and average house price data can have. (For more details refer to **Misleading or flawed data** later in this chapter.)

To my sincere disappointment though, I found that in New Zealand the HPI was only produced on a regional basis and not on a more localised basis for each suburb within a region. It seemed I was doomed to not be able to get the dial I so desperately needed to help me decide where to buy! But fortunately I persisted with my quest. I contacted the government department that produced the HPI (Quotable Value New Zealand) to see if they would consider producing a more localised equivalent of their HPI for each suburb within the regions. They advised that if I supplied them with the suitable methodology to create such an index and used qualified statisticians to 'create' it, then I could pay to use their raw data and achieve my need to more accurately measure specific suburbs' real estate price trends on an ongoing basis.

So I made the financial commitment and embarked on that mission. We created this new index and called it the 'Hybrid Index' (now SuburbWatch). The SuburbWatch was created for over eighty different suburb groupings within New Zealand's three major cities, Auckland, Wellington and Christchurch (combined population approximately 2,000,000). It was also critical to have a historic view of what had happened to real estate prices in our suburb groupings too, so we retrospectively created this real estate price indicator for the previous twelve years.

Two years and a significant financial investment later, I had my second dial. I had achieved what no one else had achieved by creating the only localised real estate price indicator in New Zealand.

It wasn't until I finally got this information that I could very clearly see the specific real estate price trends in specific suburbs and how they were somewhat interrelated to real estate price trends in the surrounding suburbs. (There are tables revealing samples of these patterns at the back of this book.)

This dial taught me how the 'ripple effect' works and, in combination with my real estate cycle dial, it also gave me some clues about how to identify cyclical hot spots.

When any suburb becomes a hot spot there is inevitably some form of 'spill over' effect on surrounding suburbs. These suburbs will benefit from some subsequent capital growth if for no other reason than the fact that they are neighbouring the suburb which is a hot spot. This does not mean that these surrounding suburbs will also become hot spots, but they will benefit from some capital growth in the short term.

It's not that the future always mimics the past, but the past can certainly provide a clear picture of what is likely to occur in the future given similar conditions to those that existed in the past. It's the same as the concept of 'cause and effect' that you learn in a chemical laboratory. Given a combination of similar ingredients and a similar environment you can expect a similar result to that previously evidenced under similar conditions.

Why you need 'special dials'

With more than twenty years' experience in the finance industry, I have seen many accomplished investors get caught out, because they failed to observe the real estate market properly; these were the same people who were very successful while the going was good. They were relying too heavily on their own visual perception. Even Donald Trump (who has always been good at buying

49

undervalued assets) admits he was billions of dollars in debt once and owed the banks too much for them to bankrupt him! He didn't read the signals of the real estate cycle and almost got wiped out as a result, despite his skills in buying undervalued assets.

It has been critical to my own wealth creation in the last five years to not only know the basics of what a good real estate deal is, but to also use my 'special dials' to assist with my real estate purchase timing and location decisions.

My 'dials' have helped me measure what 'time' the real estate cycle is experiencing compared with historical cycles, enabling me to know what is genuinely happening to real estate price trends as well as what real estate prices are likely to do in the near future. This combination has helped me to do well from real estate very safely and achieve a 'multiplication' of real estate profits since 2001. This was not luck or chance, it was because I used my 'special dials' to ascertain where and when to buy.

So my choice is to always have both sight and 'special dials' to follow. I stand by the value of rigorous and ongoing analysis. It doesn't mean such analysis is always going to be perfectly right but I would rather fly by sight *and* 'special dials' than by sight alone.

Misleading or flawed data

The direction of real estate prices (or capital growth rates) are regularly quoted in the media, but unfortunately sometimes the data relied upon can be misleading or flawed, resulting in inaccurate expectations.

There seems to be a common misperception that median or average house price data are good or accurate indicators of house price growth, but is this really true?

With respect to medians the answer depends to a degree on the volume of real estate sales that you are measuring. This is because in a large enough region (i.e. where hundreds or thousands of sales occur in any given period, i.e. per month) medians do tend to give a reasonable indication of the direction and magnitude of real estate price movements. However, when gauging real estate price movements in smaller or 'localised' areas such as individual suburbs (where perhaps less than one hundred property sales occur in any given period) the median is open to distortion due to 'compositional' factors (discussed below), which can give an incorrect indication of the direction and/or magnitude of real estate price movements.

So while median price movements can provide some useful indication of regional real estate price movements I recommend you do not rely on them when considering localised real estate price movements for individual suburbs.

The Median/Average House Price Myth = The belief that median or average house price data always provide an accurate or useful indication of house price growth.

With respect to average sales prices I would never rely on such data to ascertain the direction and/or magnitude of real estate price movements. This period's average property sale price may have been much higher than the previous period's average property sale price but just because the average price increases that does not mean values must have increased as well. No, it just means that the average price is higher than it was previously.

There is often great fanfare in the media surrounding house prices based on median house price data, including headlines like 'House prices drop $500 a day!'. Many credible sources appear to base their real estate outlook upon median figures which are subject to much distortion and can easily misrepresent house prices. While recognising the timeliness of the release of median price data, which is typically released monthly, the accuracy of the impression this data leaves can be poor and very misleading.

I also believe that average and median real estate prices are flawed in theory as well as in practice based on my observation of this data for New Zealand since the early 1990s. In the past I too used such data to help decide which suburbs I should buy property in, but eventually became astounded to find that this data can be distorted. Often locations that look like they have had little capital growth (based on median data) have actually had strong capital growth and vice versa.

The main problem with medians and averages is that they are subject to distortion by 'compositional' factors. Compositional factors include the volume of real estate sales within specific price bands. For example, if mainly low-value properties in a suburb are sold in a month (and few or none of the superior properties in that location) then this can indicate a drop in the median or average. However, in the next month most sales in that location may be superior properties (i.e. higher values) and this would then show that the median and average house price had increased when in fact values overall may have fallen.

For example, if there are eleven properties sold in a month in a suburb with most of the properties being cheaper homes and then there are eleven sales of different but generally higher-priced properties in the same location in the next month, the median and average indication of house price rises can be distorted.

PROPERTY	SALE PRICES MONTH 1	SALE PRICES MONTH 2	
Property # 1	$100,000	$120,000	
Property # 2	$120,000	$130,000	
Property # 3	$130,000	$135,000	
Property # 4	$150,000	$135,000	
Property # 5	$150,000	$140,000	
Property # 6	**$160,000**	**$195,000**	**Median**
Property # 7	$170,000	$212,000	
Property # 8	$180,000	$228,000	
Property # 9	$190,000	$238,000	
Property # 10	$200,000	$245,000	
Property # 11	$215,000	$265,000	
Median =	$160,000	$190,000	**+ 18.75%**
Average =	$160,454	$185,727	**+ 15.75%**

We know that statistically neither of these measures will give an accurate indication of capital growth, because values in the location may have actually fallen. Just because more properties sell at higher prices does not mean that values have increased, even though the average and median data will imply that is what has occurred. It is this 'compositional' error that makes median and average house price data worthless in the context of measuring real estate capital growth rates on a localised basis where there are inadequate sales to justify a reliable median measurement.

In contrast, House Price Indices are based on actual sales data compared with a consistent benchmark which is not solely the previous month's sales data. A suitable benchmark used in some countries has been the value applied to each property for the purposes of assessing a 'rateable' value. Typically such a value is used to determine local council costs or government taxes on each property. While it is acknowledged that these 'rateable' values are not necessarily a clear representation of the true market value of each property, they can be used as an accurate benchmark to measure capital growth rates.

Some indices also rely on resale data (i.e. comparing the sale price of a property with the price when the same property was last sold) and these indices also tend to produce good-quality information which can be relied on. The quality of such indices will be largely determined by the volume of data within the database which is being used to determine the percentage movements in the index. In the event the data represents only 10 per cent of property sales within a location then the quality of the index would be poor compared to an index based on every sale within that location which would give the most accurate index.

It is not just my own opinion that House Price Indices provide the most accurate house price growth data available; this opinion is shared by other real estate market observers. Internationally, experts acknowledge that House Price Indices generally provide the most accurate house price measure. Even major publications such as *The Economist* now utilise House Price Indices to quote house price growth rates, rather than using median or average house price data.

So be extremely careful when making real estate purchase or sale decisions based on historic or forecast capital growth. If you are making a large financial commitment to buy a property then at least make sure you are not relying on flawed data to assist your decision. Do as much of your own 'homework' on values and rents as you can before purchasing to ensure you minimise your risks. (See Chapter 4.)

How to spot self-interested media releases announcing real estate hot spots

There are many media reports about the latest real estate hot spots all around the world and most of these are sourced directly from the local real estate industry players. This is in itself no surprise as the people within the real estate industry are often the most qualified people to make such a 'call'. Unfortunately, though, all too often these press releases are issued to actually support the creation of a hot spot based on local opinion that the location has great potential for one reason or another. Perhaps it's simply because the location is beside the sea (a large portion of the world is!), or there is some other equally compelling reason why the local industry players are convinced the location will achieve strong capital growth.

The press releases issued by self-interested people usually lack facts and allude to vague statements about the location like:

1. A growing number of people are moving into the location. While an increasing population is a key to increased demand, the questions that need to be answered are these:

   ▶ How many people are actually moving into a suburb or location in relation to how many properties are actually being built?
   If 1000 people are moving into a suburb or location a month but developers are building enough properties to house 2000 people per month then a hot spot can quickly become a cold spot (producing negative capital growth).

   ▶ What has been the historic trend of population growth in the location and why?
   If there have been historic surges in population growth, why have they occurred and have they proved sustainable? Extreme historic examples of surges in population growth

followed by a collapse of that population would be the
hundreds (or more) of 'ghost towns' around the world
that were once thriving towns. Some of these towns grew
rapidly as a result of a gold rush only to turn into ghost
towns once the gold ran out or there were better prospects
found elsewhere.

The same pattern is set to reoccur in some real estate
markets as some developments (in particular those in
remote locations with insufficient infrastructure) will
be abandoned by developers who go broke when the
population growth tap is turned off or, worse still, there
is a rapid and mass exodus of occupants. The first real
estate boom of the new millennium is set to leave behind
a plethora of abandoned or half-completed developments
when the tide turns on the international real estate market.
It would not even take a real estate bubble burst or
international real estate crash to result in such a legacy.
Instead it will only need an oversupply of real estate, a
decrease in demand, or both, in some of the locations
currently being touted as real estate hot spots.

2. The climate is fantastic here.

    ▶ Are there other 'competing' locations relatively nearby
      with a similar or better climate and superior amenities or
      commerce? Of course a great climate can be magnificent
      for maintaining strong demand for a location. However,
      there are many locations with great climates so the price
      premium that real estate buyers are prepared to pay to
      live in a location with a great climate is limited. Limited
      because there is always a choice of locations and always
      some 'newly discovered' location with a great climate.
      These newly discovered locations are often the result of

improved access to the location and investment in local
infrastructure, not just the climate.

3. You need very little cash to acquire real estate here.

▶ This is not a sound reason in itself for a real estate hot spot
to emerge because the amount of cash needed to acquire
real estate will only have a short-term and limited impact
on the level of demand for real estate. Consider what
would happen if everyone could borrow 100 per cent of
the purchase price of real estate. The net effect of such
'easy money' would initially result in a surge of demand.
However, this surge would not be sustained if the interest
and ownership costs of owning the real estate were greater
than the cost of renting an equivalent property. This would
limit the number of people prepared to buy because renting
would be more cost effective in comparison and ownership
would bring a financial burden.

Real estate investors would also have a limited capacity
to accumulate properties because every time they bought
another property it would have a negative impact on their
cash flow position. They do not buy every property they
come across simply because they have access to the funds
to do so. Typically, every time an investor buys another
property their *ongoing* financial commitment also
increases.

4. We have great tourism prospects.

▶ Are there 'competing' tourism destinations that are
superior or similar but offering better value?
Usually the promoter of such a 'tourism prospect'
destination will be biased and often will make assumptions
about the superiority of the location they are promoting.
There are plenty of tourism destinations in the world to

choose from and these markets can be fickle with large surges in supply and demand creating volatile values.

5. We are developing the location at a rapid rate.

▶ Overdevelopment is exactly why a location will not *remain* a hot spot and rapid development will not ensure any location will *become* a hot spot. While the reasons above may be influencing demand for a location, you actually need to consider the longer-term trends to really be able to assess whether a suburb or location is going to become or continue to be a real estate hot spot or not. The analysis in the next chapter of what actually causes a hot spot to emerge will go some way towards helping you decipher the self-interested press releases from the genuine ones.

Chapter Summary

▶ Special dials can assist your real estate investment decision-making.

▶ While median price movements can provide some useful indication of regional property price movements they should not be relied on when considering localised property price movements for individual suburbs.

▶ Average sales prices should not be relied on to ascertain the direction and/or magnitude of property price movements.

▶ Press releases are often issued to actually support the creation of a hot spot and can be based on self-interested opinion.

3

What Drives Hot Spots to Emerge?

- ▶ Supply and demand
- ▶ The hot spots mantra
- ▶ 'Rear view mirror' research
- ▶ Introduction to the hot spot drivers
- ▶ Drilling down to the details
- ▶ Hot spot drivers checklist
- ▶ Hot spot driver contradictions

Supply and demand

A rapid and significant increase in demand for any location will quickly boost real estate values, just as a sharp and significant decrease in demand will quickly reduce values.

Hot spots emerge when the supply of real estate in a location is limited and the demand is high and cold spots emerge when the demand for real estate is low and the supply of real estate is plentiful. This chapter focuses on hot spot drivers not cold spot drivers, because cold spots are driven by an absence of these hot spot drivers.

The emergence of a hot spot typically occurs rapidly. The underlying reasons for the emergence of a hot spot, though, can sometimes be the result of slow and seemingly insignificant changes which incrementally bring about the perfect environment for exponential and rapid change.

Malcolm Gladwell describes the complex dynamics that cause rapid change in his international bestseller *The Tipping Point*. Gladwell explains how little things can sometimes make a huge difference to create a 'tipping point' when massive change occurs. He says, 'There are times when we need a convenient shortcut, a way to make a lot out of a little, and that is what Tipping Points, in the end, are all about.'

I believe the dynamics of tipping points equally apply to what cause real estate hot spots to emerge, because small changes can collectively make a huge difference to the levels of supply and demand for real estate within any specific location, resulting in a surge in values in a short space of time. If we can identify the tipping points that cause real estate hot spots to emerge then we have a convenient shortcut, a way to make a lot out of a little.

By default the supply of real estate is always limited to some degree by the number of properties available for sale, or available to be built for sale in any given location. This level of supply tends to change slowly initially because of the lead-in time for additional properties to be built. Generally, new buildings have a long lead-in time because of the time involved in the building approval process combined with the time it takes to build.

While the supply of real estate is always limited to some degree, there are a few impacting factors that can significantly affect the level of supply.

▶ Land availability – However, bear in mind the ability for 'fields' land to be created (as discussed in the next few pages).

▶ Amended zoning for intensification – If regulations or restrictions on building are amended to allow more buildings or dwellings to be built, the level of supply will increase.

▶ Economic viability of building – If it is cheaper to build than to buy an existing building, you can expect more buildings to be built, therefore increasing the level of supply.

In contrast, demand can be impacted by many factors, often at the same time, and, in light of the restriction on supply, strongly increased demand will create pressure on potential buyers to pay ever-increasing prices until they reach a level no one is prepared to pay.

But we need to consider much more than just the level of supply and demand because short-term, temporary swings in demand can sometimes give the illusion that a hot spot may occur when in fact such value growth may be limited and prove unsustainable in the short term.

Real estate values will continue to rise in the event demand remains significantly higher than the level of supply. Of course, the opposite also applies when there is too much supply and not enough demand, typically resulting in sharp decreases in real estate values as more and more people try to sell to a limited pool of potential purchasers. In particular, poor-quality real estate will be likely to suffer the largest decrease in value as these properties typically appeal to real estate investors who have no emotional attachment to the property and, therefore, no emotional premium in the price they are prepared to pay for it.

The hot spots mantra – research, research, research

The old real estate mantra of location, location, location has proven to have little, if any, validity when you are looking for real estate hot spots. Just because a suburb is superior to its surrounding suburbs does not guarantee it will experience strong capital growth.

My new real estate mantra is research, research, research because that is the key to locating a hot spot, not just its location.

To be able to pinpoint locations that will become hot spots you will need to do plenty of research and fact gathering. Today, consumers are better equipped to undertake research on matters relating to real estate than they ever have been, because the Internet offers the opportunity to access data and information that just ten years ago was unavailable to them.

The research you will need to undertake to identify hot spots and minimise your risk of investing includes considering historic trends as well as assessing current trends of the hot spot drivers.

'Rear view mirror' research

Rear view mirror research is exactly what the term implies: looking back. Looking back at the past to consider what has historically driven demand for people to occupy the location.

While history does not necessarily repeat, it can sometimes give a good indication of why things are the way they are today, and what may occur tomorrow. Historic trends can give you an indication of what might impact on demand in the location in the future, based on what has impacted on demand in the past. It will help to know as much about the background history of a location as you can.

So when you find a location you think is or will be a hot spot make sure you take a look in the 'rear view mirror'.

Rear view mirror research is to obtain an overview of the location's past. Here is your rear view mirror checklist:

▶ Background information like the various eras and styles of dwelling, the occupants who typically live there and why they choose to live there is important so you can understand what is motivating or possibly could motivate demand to occupy the location.

▶ What events have historically had a significant impact on values, how much was the impact and how long did it last?

▶ Is the local economy reliant on the viability of a single industry or resource? If so, how have changing economic times affected real estate values?

The answers to these questions will form a view of the history of the location and highlight potential opportunity and some of the potential risks too.

This rear view mirror research creates the foundation to which you can add your more recent research. This combination of history and the present can bring fresh insights which highlight opportunity and signals of risk.

Introduction to the hot spot drivers

My research into hot spots indicates there are some common drivers of demand, which I call hot spot drivers. Equally, an absence of these drivers is likely to indicate a cold spot delivering negative capital growth.

It is unlikely that any single hot spot driver will create the perfect environment for the emergence of a hot spot. It is much more likely for several hot spot drivers to be collectively responsible for creating a hot spot just as an absence of these drivers can indicate the potential for a cold spot.

The more hot spot drivers that exist within a location, the more likely that it will become a real estate hot spot.

If there is a distinct absence of drivers then it is more likely to become a real estate cold spot.

These drivers are either demographic, geographic, social, economic or real estate market based. Some of these categories will demonstrate hot spot drivers early on in the progress of a hot spot and others will only become evident after a hot spot has emerged. The categories that demonstrate hot spot drivers early are demographic, geographic and social. In contrast, the economic and real estate market drivers only become evident as a result of the former drivers. They can all impact on the level of demand and supply in any location. Sometimes many small collective adjustments in various drivers will hint at a hot spot's emergence, so it makes sense to consider them carefully.

Hot spot drivers – drilling down to the details

Some of the hot spot drivers are easy to recognise while others will require close observation. In this chapter you will find a checklist of the hot spot drivers that you can use to record which drivers exist in any given location. The data and information required to assess a location's likelihood of becoming a hot spot will probably need to come from many different sources. Try to ensure the data is from reliable sources and, preferably, independent of anyone with a vested interest in misrepresenting the data. When it is not possible to source independent data, for example, you may get data about real estate sales in the location from a realtor who has a vested interest in selling you a property, then seek out similar data from several sources. If you source such data from six different realtors in the location then you will most likely get a better insight into any inconsistencies in the supplied data and, therefore, reduce the risk of any misrepresentation influencing your decisions.

Never act on hearsay alone. Do your own homework to ensure any decision can be justified with facts and figures.

No matter how many hot spot drivers are apparent you will still need to make sure you are not paying too much for any properties you buy in the first place. The old adage 'You make your money when you buy' still applies to buying in real estate hot spots. Again, you will need to do your homework in this respect, and research sales of comparable properties in the location.

Below is a brief list by category of the various drivers which bode well for the emergence of a hot spot. Following this list are more detailed explanations of the specific hot spot driver *categories* and *drivers*.

List of hot spot drivers
Demographic Drivers

▶ **Population increase** is strong. A population growth rate in excess of 1 per cent per annum is considered conducive to supporting hot spots.

▶ **New/significantly improved amenities.** Large-scale new or improved amenities.

▶ **Zoning amended for intensification.** Locations which are newly rezoned for intensification.

- Strong employment growth.
- Market segment demand is surging.

Geographic Drivers

- **Transport links** or access to the location is new/improved.
- **Inferior locations bordering highly desirable locations** which are experiencing strong growth.
- **Amenities proximity.** Seek out locations which are well located but have had little or no growth compared to surrounding locations.
- **Waterfront location** with little or no growth compared to surrounding locations.

Social Drivers

- **Renamed suburb**, especially if the suburb has also shown a major crime reduction.
- **New/improved schooling.**
- **Major reduction in crime.**
- **Café set.** Seek out locations where 'trendy' cafés are being opened.
- **Artists and authors** moving into a location.
- A **major deterioration in security**, resulting in increased demand for bolthole locations.
- **Improved visual appeal.** Seek out locations with visual appeal that have been overlooked by others.
- **Trendiness increasing.**
- **Architecture and gentrification.** Consider the architecture of a location and its potential for significant gentrification. Seek out locations with character and style which is yet to be realised.

Economic Drivers

▶ **Strong rental demand** and sharp rises in rents.

▶ **Affordability improving**.

▶ **Real estate values increasing**. When values increase by more than 4 per cent in a single quarter or by more than 8 per cent in two consecutive quarters this is a good indicator of a cyclical hot spot.

▶ **Urban renewal/demolition of derelict buildings** on a significant scale.

▶ **Yields increasing strongly**.

▶ **Rapid economic growth or expansion**.

Real Estate Market Drivers

▶ **Time to sell** is rapidly reducing.

▶ **Real estate sales volumes increasing rapidly**.

▶ **Average ownership timeframe reducing rapidly**.

▶ **Multiple offers on properties**.

▶ **Shortage of available properties**.

Now we take a detailed look at the various categories and drivers which influence the emergence of real estate hot spots.

Demographic Drivers

Demographic drivers are those demographics which fundamentally increase the level of demand to occupy a suburb or location. Remember these drivers are efficient early indicators of possible hot spots.

▶ **Population increase is strong. Population = (births – deaths) + (immigrants – emigrants)**. Immigrants include those who move to the location from overseas and from other parts of the same country. Emigrants include those who move out of the location to overseas or other parts of the same country. A natural population increase from births exceeding deaths takes time to filter into an increased need for housing, because typically having a child does not create an instant need for more housing, therefore a natural population increase is not usually adequate to create a hot spot. Particularly strong net migration, however, can occur quickly at times and this strong net migration bodes very well for the emergence of a hot spot. *A population growth rate in excess of 1 per cent per annum is considered conducive to supporting hot spots.*

▶ **New/significantly improved amenities.** Such amenities include those which cater for 'emerging' needs. For example, the increasing health needs of baby boomers mean they will demand to live in close proximity to modern hospital or medical facilities. So a new hospital or even a significantly improved one will increase demand for people to live nearby. Other new/improved amenities which can help a hot spot to emerge can range from new/significantly improved tertiary education facilities to a new/significantly improved large-scale shopping mall.

The principle of 'bigger is better' applies in relation to amenities because the bigger the scale of new or improved amenities the more attractive the location will become for occupants. *Therefore, large-scale new or improved amenities bode well for the emergence of a hot spot.* Bear in mind that once construction of the amenities is completed they are no longer considered to be a hot spot driver because demand usually peaks before construction is completed.

▶ **Zoning amended for intensification.** Look for locations which are soon to be rezoned to allow for an increase in the number of households per site. Such rezoning typically emanates from local government bodies so it pays to stay in touch with any proposed amendments. Buying as soon as the amendment is approved will help you to maximise the capital growth which will become apparent once everyone realises the new zoning applies and that it has effectively increased the value of existing properties. Be cautious of buying in any locations that are proposed to have a zone change but have not actually had the change approved. Even though you will make more money if you buy before any zone change is approved, you also increase your risk substantially because the location may not be subsequently approved for rezoning! *Locations which are newly rezoned for intensification can emerge into hot spots.*

▶ **Employment growth is strong**. The arrival of a significant new employer nearby will always attract new occupants and increase the demand for real estate in the location. *Strong employment growth bodes well for a location to become a hot spot.*

▶ **Market segment demand is surging**. Which market segment is the surge in demand coming from? For example, is it empty nesters (those who no longer have children living at home) who can finally pursue their desire of living in a low-maintenance property that is conveniently located? Other market segments can include professionals, factory workers, miners, fishermen, celebrities, business owners, students, sea changers (retirees seeking to live near the sea) or any concentration of people with similar needs, and typically at a similar stage in life. Often those in a market segment are in the same generation, too, such as sea changers who are typically baby boomers. There are also market segments comprising groups of people sharing a common socio-economic status or accommodation niche, such as student housing, holiday accommodation and serviced apartments. If the demand surge is a result of a surge for a niche accommodation type, which mainly suits a specific type of tenant, be aware that sometimes these surges can be very strong, but also short-term, resulting in a potentially higher volatility of values.

A market segment-driven surge in demand can contribute to a hot spot's emergence.

Demographic Driver Secrets

Observe the demographic drivers and learn to recognise their collective impact on real estate values, as demographic drivers are early indicators of possible hot spots.

Geographic drivers

Not all land is equal. Some of the best land in the world is not in demand and almost worthless! But some of the worst land in the world is very expensive. This is simply because the value of land lies in its value to the people occupying it. And that value is often influenced by geographic elements. For example, a location may be very desirable but if it is inaccessible then that value is diminished. Hence a new transport link giving access to that previously inaccessible but desirable location can create the perfect environment for a hot spot to develop. Geographic drivers relate to some geographic feature of the location. Bear in mind that some geographic features can be man-made. Remember geographic drivers are efficient early indicators of possible hot spots. Here are the geographic clues to the next real estate hot spot:

▶ **Transport links or access** to the location is new/improved. This is a good indicator if commuting time to the nearest main centre is significantly reduced by the new transport link and/or access way. *New/improved transport links and access bode well for the emergence of a hot spot.*

▶ **Inferior location bordering highly desirable locations.** Inferior locations which have yet to experience much capital growth but which are bordering superior locations that have already experienced strong capital growth (i.e. the bordering location/s have had 10 per cent or more capital growth in the preceding six months) have the potential to become hot spots. *An inferior location bordering highly desirable locations that are experiencing strong growth bodes well for the emergence of a hot spot.*

▶ **Amenities proximity.** Sometimes locations that are in close proximity to highly sought-after amenities (like large shopping malls, an entertainment district or public amenities) are much cheaper than surrounding locations. However, if the surrounding locations experience strong capital growth then the cheaper locations should experience at least some capital growth. *Seek out locations which are well located but have had little or no growth compared to surrounding locations. These locations increase the likelihood of a hot spot emerging.*

▶ **Waterfront.** A waterfront location in itself will not guarantee the location will become a hot spot. However, if the location has experienced inferior capital growth compared with the locations surrounding it then its natural features, such as fronting onto water, may have been undervalued. *Seek out locations which are waterfront but have had little or no growth compared to surrounding locations. These locations increase the likelihood of a hot spot emerging.*

Geographic Driver Secrets

Buy in suburbs about to benefit from significant new/ improved transport links, in particular if these suburbs are adjacent to a suburb having significant value added to it. Geographic drivers are early indicators of possible hot spots.

Social drivers

Social drivers are hard to measure because they cannot be easily quantified. For example, how do you measure the level of a location's trendiness? Or how visually appealing a location is when people have different opinions on what is appealing?

Social driver influences on hot spots are very much the result of public perception. We know that certain changes in a location will adjust the general public perception of that location, for example, if a significant reduction in crime can be achieved then the desirability of that location will improve. So the social drivers are those that change perceptions which fundamentally increase the level of demand to occupy a location.

Remember social drivers are efficient early indicators of possible hot spots. Here are the social clues to the next real estate hot spot:

▶ **Renamed suburb**. Suburbs are renamed for various reasons such as undergoing urban renewal or large-scale gentrification, or to reflect the emergence of a 'new' suburb to replace an old one which may have had a bad or dangerous reputation. Often renamed suburbs have previously had high unemployment or have been a slum with poorly maintained dwellings suffering from overcrowding, drugs and crime.

These locations sometimes have a high density of population per square kilometre and poorly planned developments. When a location has become a slum or 'crime capital' (i.e. experiencing a high level of crime) but then undergoes large-scale urban renewal or gentrification, it is usually accompanied by a concerted and significant 'crime clean-up'. This can give the suburb a fresh reputation with a new focus. Typically, when new or replacement dwellings are built they will cater to different occupants than those who previously lived there, and the price range of these new properties typically prohibits many former occupants from living there. *The renaming of a neighbourhood can create the perfect environment for a hot spot to emerge, especially if the suburb has also shown a major crime reduction.*

- **New/improved schooling**. When schooling improves so too does the level of disposable income entering that local economy. Schooling generates employment, delivers a better quality of new employees, lifts local morale and reduces crime rates. This is all good for local real estate values over time but a location has a better chance of becoming a hot spot prior to completion of the new/improved school. Once construction is completed demand should already have peaked and values in the location will already have risen. *New/improved schooling can influence the emergence of a hot spot.*

- **Major reduction in crime**. If crime can be minimised then real estate values can be maximised. Imagine if you could put a price on living in a low crime location compared with a high crime one. What is the value of providing a safer living environment for your family? So, if the price premium for better schooling can be in the tens of thousands of dollars or more, is your family's safety worth more? Of course it is, in fact their safety is probably worth a lot more! For signs of crime look for how much graffiti exists in the location – the more graffiti, generally, the more crime. *A major crime reduction can support the emergence of a hot spot.*

» **Café set.** The café set is the term given to those who frequent cafés on a regular basis and most often in or near the location they live in. Typically the café set emerge as a result of an increase in the number of people with above-average wealth for the location moving into the location. Therefore new cafés opening can signal a hot spot emerging. *Seek out locations where 'trendy' cafés are being opened. This can be an early indicator of a hot spot emerging.*

» **Artists and authors arriving.** Artists and authors like to be surrounded by things that give them inspiration. They like buildings with redeeming architectural features and big open spaces so they can have plenty of 'creative space' to work within. Perhaps the location has recently had a crime clean-up, but demolition is not yet a viable proposition or is tied up in a lengthy bureaucratic process of approval. Many buildings in the location will be in a state of disrepair. So redevelopment will not yet be occurring en masse. Many buildings will have some architectural interest. This combination of relative safety, 'creative' space and architectural interest is what attracts artists to the location. *Look for where the 'arty' types are moving to, because they are often the first ones to move to locations that are emerging as trendy places to live and, thus, are likely to become hot spots.*

» **A major deterioration in security, resulting in increased demand for bolthole locations.** A bolthole is a safe haven location. Somewhere that is perceived to be very safe from acts of war and violence. We know security has a value because properties in low crime locations command a price premium to some degree. The degree of this price premium is likely to be exaggerated in the event of a major shock such as a major terrorist attack. *In times of turbulent security expect bolthole locations to benefit from a surge in demand. This can contribute to a hot spot emerging.*

- **Improved visual appeal**. Sometimes a location can improve its visual appeal over time. Take, for example, a neighbourhood overlooking an industrial area with a one-year-old forest planted between the neighbourhood and the industrial centre. Come back in ten years when the trees have blocked out the view of the industrial area and the outlook has become more visually appealing! Of course, what constitutes visual appeal may differ as it is based on personal opinion. Often these locations will be overlooked by people who remember only the original appearance of the location. *Seek out locations with visual appeal overlooked by others.*

- **Trendiness increasing**. It never ceases to amaze me how formerly 'tired' suburbs can suddenly be considered a trendy place to live. Suburbs become trendy if they house popular food, fashion and entertainment venues, as dictated by public perception. To assess trendiness you will need some local knowledge which can be obtained by visiting shops, cafés and entertainment venues in the location. Realtors/real estate agents can also give you some insight into any changes in perception of the location and why that change is taking place. *Seek out locations which are becoming more trendy as this can sometimes be an early signal of a hot spot.*

- **Architecture and gentrification**. In my home town of Auckland, New Zealand, we have a well-located city fringe suburb called Ponsonby. In the early 1900s, Ponsonby was settled and many grand villas were built there as well as bungalows for those not so financially well-off. The problem was that these architecturally characterful buildings required high ongoing levels of maintenance and eventually properties inevitably fell into a state of disrepair. This attracted large volumes of tenants seeking cheap but convenient accommodation close to the city centre, which was the commercial and entertainment heart of Auckland City. Eventually, most of Ponsonby became very run down. Then something changed. In the 1970s villas became trendy again and much admired for their architectural features and of course Ponsonby was ripe for redevelopment because of its significant number of character villas and bungalows. So, many were bought to be renovated and then onsold for a profit. It seemed like whole streets were being renovated one house at a time. In the 1980s many of these villas benefited from gentrification and/or a complete restoration back to their former splendour which significantly increased demand to occupy these properties and values surged in growth. *Consider the architecture of a location and its potential for significant gentrification.* If most of the properties in the location were restored to their former glory would the location ooze character and charm? Or is the architecture of the location now back in vogue or trendy? *Seek out locations with character and style which is yet to be realised.*

Social Driver Secrets

Know who is buying and who is selling real estate and why. Learn how such buyers and sellers have historically impacted on real estate values in the local area. Social drivers are early indicators of possible hot spots.

Economic drivers

To real estate *investors*, the value of real estate is based mainly on the return it can produce for the investor. The higher the return or the desire for people to occupy the location, the higher the value.

In contrast, those purchasing real estate to live in *themselves* typically have scant regard for the economic return from owning it. They are more interested in the demographic, geographic and social issues of the location they wish to live in. The main economic driver to concern them will be the level of affordability.

Economic drivers typically only become evident as a result of the effects of the demographic, geographic and social drivers. Economic drivers can also reveal the ripple effect in action, allowing you to buy in front of the ripple if you have good data on the economic drivers. Remember economic drivers are efficient mid to late indicators of hot spots. Below are the economic clues to the next real estate hot spot:

▶ **Strong rental demand.** In the event of overwhelming demand for housing rents can quickly spiral upwards which can be a great sign of an emerging hot spot. But you need to consider whether such strong demand is likely to continue or is just a temporary demand, so you need to ask what has created the surge in rents. Was it some temporary 'blip' in demand or was there a more lasting reason for the increase? For example, if such demand is on the back of a large, but one-off sports event such as hosting the America's Cup yacht races then the surge is unlikely to prove sustainable and after the sports event finishes rents are likely to reduce significantly. If the surge in rents is caused by some one-off event then be cautious about expecting to be able to profit from the location's capital growth as such growth is likely to be factored into real estate prices very quickly initially (possibly even before the venue is confirmed as the host for the sports event).

However, if the surge is on the back of a genuine tenant demand driven by a combination of other economic hot spot drivers, such rental increases are likely to be sustainable. In that case you can capitalise on the location as a hot spot because generally rents lead values, so if rents increase rapidly then soon after values will also increase. *Seek out locations experiencing sharp rises in rents as this can indicate a hot spot.*

▸ **Affordability improving**. Real estate affordability is impacted by many different factors such as interest rates, real estate values and even by financiers' lending policies. However, the funny thing about affordability is that it's not the sort of indicator that most people watch very closely. In reality real estate can quickly become less (or more) affordable, but most people will be slower to update their perception of how affordable it is. *The more affordable real estate is, the more likely the location is to emerge as a hot spot.*

▸ **Real estate values increasing**. Values are not necessarily a good hot spot driver at first glance because generally they will not reveal a consistent increase until the location has already become a hot spot! However, following the trends of real estate values over time can give excellent clues of a cyclical hot spot emerging.

The locations graphed below all emerged as cyclical hot spots in the recovery or early- to mid-boom phase of the real estate cycle and all showed an initial precursor to strong growth which was either a single quarter growth rate of more than 4 per cent, or more than 8 per cent growth in two consecutive quarters. (Refer to table of SuburbWatch Movements at the end of the book for raw data.)

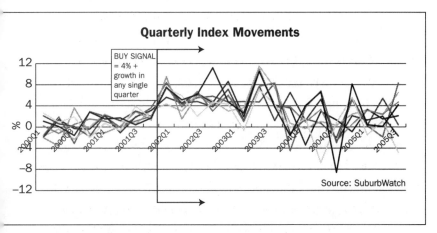

Graph 3.1

In the event a location experiences either growth and the real estate cycle is in the recovery or early- to mid-boom phase, then the location is likely to remain or become a cyclical hot spot for the next six to twelve months, or longer.

Warning: This is typically not the case if the real estate cycle is in the mid- to late-boom phase or the slump phase.

▶ **Urban renewal/demolition of derelict buildings on a significant scale.** If a location is undergoing significant urban renewal (new properties are being built to replace older ones) or the demolition of derelict buildings, then it has the potential to become a hot spot. Typically demand will be created by a strong marketing campaign by the developers of the renewed or newly-built properties. *Seek out locations about to undergo significant urban renewal as this bodes well for a hot spot to emerge.*

▶ **Yields increasing strongly.** Yields are calculated by dividing the potential rental income of a property by the purchase price of that property. The higher the yield the more upward pressure on values. Yields increase when rents rise without an accompanying rise in value. Because rent rises are often cyclical (arriving during the real estate cycle's recovery or boom phases), yields increase cyclically and, therefore, *an increase in yields can be a good way to identify cyclical hot spots.*

▶ **Economic growth or expansion is rapid.** Rapid economic growth leads to a surge of people with available funds seeking a safe investment vehicle. Real estate is the early benefactor of such wealth, not least due to the perceived safety of investing in real estate. *In the event of strong and rapid local economic growth, real estate values typically benefit relatively quickly.*

Economic Driver Secrets

Economic drivers can quickly influence the emergence of hot spots and should be closely monitored. They can reveal the ripple effect in action so are useful when investing in cyclical hot spots. Economic drivers are mid to late indicators of possible hot spots.

Real estate market drivers

The real estate market can be fickle and change fortunes quickly. A lot of emotion is attached to money, so with large financial decisions being made regularly in real estate it's no wonder the industry is an emotional one. Real estate market drivers typically only become evident after the emergence of demographic, geographic and social drivers, and as a result of them.

Remember real estate market drivers are efficient mid to late indicators of hot spots. Below are the real estate market clues to the next real estate hot spot:

▶ **Time to sell is rapidly reducing**. Has the number of days taken to sell properties in the location decreased markedly? How many days was it taking to sell properties three months ago compared to this month? The longer it takes to sell real estate, the less upward pressure there is on values, conversely the quicker real estate sells, the more upward pressure on values. This is simply because time works against sellers but in favour of buyers – there are always some sellers who *must* sell (e.g. due to financial pressure, marital separation, etc.), but few buyers must buy! If properties were selling in fifty days on average three months ago but now are selling in less than thirty, then there may well be a hot spot emerging. The key for assessing the 'time to sell' driver is in its trend. The trend of the time to sell will rapidly decrease as a hot spot emerges. Be aware that there is usually a seasonal fluctuation in the number of days to sell (i.e. in winter it may take longer to sell properties) so it is important to assess this data for at least the last two to three years so you can identify any seasonal patterns emerging. *Look for locations where the number of days to sell is rapidly reducing.*

▶ **Real estate sales volumes are increasing rapidly**. How many properties have sold in the location in the past and how many have been sold more recently (i.e. in the last month or two)? Are sales volumes rapidly increasing? Hot spots will typically demonstrate a sudden and sharp increase in sales volumes initially. Be aware that there are usually seasonal fluctuations in real estate sales volumes too (i.e. in winter there may be fewer properties sold). You don't want to confuse any seasonal volume increase as the result of a hot spot driver, so assess this data from at least the previous two to three years so you can identify any previous seasonal patterns. *If sales volumes increase rapidly, values will increase, and sometimes they will rapidly increase.*

▸ **Average ownership timeframe is reducing rapidly**. It will also assist to identify the average ownership timeframe in the location. Generally, the shorter the average ownership timeframe, the higher the demand for real estate. Compare what percentage of properties in the location have typically sold historically. Compare this with how many have been selling recently. For example, if there are typically fifty property sales per month out of a total of 6000 dwellings in the location then that represents 10 per cent of all properties selling per annum, or an average ownership period of ten years per dwelling. However, if there are one hundred property sales per month then that represents 20 per cent of all properties selling per annum or an average ownership period of just five years. *A rapid reduction in the average ownership timeframe is a sign that the location may be emerging as a hot spot.*

▸ **Multiple offers are common.** When a hot spot is emerging many potential buyers will be competing for the same properties at the same time. Often it seems like every property you consider buying already has someone else interested in it and you are faced with making a competing offer to attempt to buy the property. Sometimes this competitive market will even result in properties selling for an amount that is higher than the original asking price. Of course, in some countries properties are only sold in this manner in which case multiple offers are not a hot spot driver, but in countries where this is just one of several methods of selling real estate then multiple offers becoming common is a clear signal of a hot spot's emergence. *Multiple offers can be a sign that the location has already emerged as a hot spot.*

▶ **Shortage of available properties**. Is there an insufficient volume of properties available for sale? *When there is a shortage of properties available to sell, values will rise and a hot spot may emerge.*

Real Estate Market Driver Secrets

Real estate market drivers can quickly influence the emergence of hot spots and should be closely monitored. They too can reveal the ripple effect in action so are useful when investing in cyclical hot spots. Real estate market drivers are mid to late indicators of possible hot spots.

Hot spot drivers checklist

To ascertain whether a location is likely to be a hot spot, consider the following hot spot drivers and tick the boxes for the drivers that are evident in the location. Detailed explanations of each driver follow in the pages after this checklist.

The hot spot drivers are divided into categories. Next to each driver is a possible early indicator that can sometimes let you know rapid change is about to occur as well as likely sources of data and information for assessing hot spots.

DRIVER	POSSIBLE EARLY INDICATOR	LIKELY SOURCE OF DATA/ INFORMATION
Demographic		
☐ Population increases	Local government body policy change	Government statistics or news websites
☐ New/improved amenities	Local government body project approval	Local governing council or news websites
☐ Zoning amended for intensification	Local government body policy change	Local governing council or news websites
☐ Employment growth	Local government body project approval	Government statistics or news websites
☐ Market segment demand	Population shifts/ age range/socio- economic status	Government statistics or news websites
Geographic		
☐ New/improved transport links	Local government body project approval	Local governing council or news websites
☐ Inferior location bordering highly desirable areas	Real estate cycle recovery/boom phases	Realtors/real estate agents
☐ Amenities proximity	Real estate cycle boom phase	Mapping websites or local knowledge
☐ Waterfront	Real estate cycle boom phase	Mapping websites or local knowledge
Social		
☐ Renamed neighbourhood	Local government body project approval	Local governing council or news websites
☐ New/improved schooling	Local government body project approval	Local governing council or news websites

WHAT DRIVES HOT SPOTS TO EMERGE?

DRIVER	POSSIBLE EARLY INDICATOR	LIKELY SOURCE OF DATA/ INFORMATION
Social cont.		
☐ Major reduction in crime	Local government body policy change	Local police or news websites
☐ Café set	Increase in occupants' wealth	Realtors/real estate agents, visit cafés
☐ Artists and authors arriving	Increase in trendiness	Realtors/real estate agents, visit cafés
☐ Security (bolthole)	International unrest due to terrorism, war	News websites
☐ Visual appeal improved	Local government body project approval	Drive around the location
☐ Trendiness improvement	Changing public perception	Drive around the location, realtors/real estate agents, visit cafés
☐ Architecture lends itself to restoration	Local government body policy change	Drive around the location
☐ Gentrification is rapidly increasing		Drive around the location
Economic		
☐ Rental demand strong	Real estate cycle recovery phase	Realtors/real estate agents, real estate statistics websites
☐ Affordability improving	Real estate cycle late in the slump phase	Real estate statistics websites
☐ Real estate values increasing	Real estate cycle recovery phase	Realtors/real estate agents, real estate statistics websites
☐ Urban renewal/ demolition of derelict buildings is significant	Real estate cycle boom phase	Local governing council or news websites
☐ Yields increasing rapidly	Real estate cycle recovery phase	Realtors/real estate agents, real estate statistics websites
☐ Economic growth is rapid	Real estate cycle recovery phase	News websites

DRIVER	POSSIBLE EARLY INDICATOR	LIKELY SOURCE OF DATA/ INFORMATION
Real estate market		
☐ Time to sell reducing rapidly	Real estate cycle recovery phase	Realtors/real estate agents, real estate statistics websites
☐ Real estate sales volumes increasing rapidly	Real estate cycle recovery phase	Realtors/real estate agents, real estate statistics websites
☐ Average ownership timeframe reducing rapidly	Real estate cycle recovery phase	Realtors/real estate agents, real estate statistics websites
☐ Multiple offers are common	Real estate cycle recovery phase	Realtors/real estate agents
☐ Shortage of available properties	Real estate cycle boom phase	Realtors/real estate agents

How many hot spot drivers are needed to create a hot spot?

It is difficult to identify the exact number of drivers needed for hot spots because a hot spot can emerge as a result of just one significant change such as a population growth surge. However, I have assessed what type of hot spot exists based on the number of hot spot drivers influencing the location. This is not to be taken as absolute but as an indication only.

The following is my indicative assessment of the most likely number of drivers to identify certain types of hot spots:

Possible – five or more demographic/geographic/social drivers

Likely – seven or more demographic/geographic/social drivers (preferably a minimum of one in each category)

Emerging – ten or more demographic/geographic/social drivers *and* three or more economic/real estate market drivers

Existing – ten or more demographic/geographic/social drivers *and* five or more economic/real estate market drivers

Cyclical – The real estate cycle will be in either the recovery or boom phase with three or more economic and/or real estate market drivers but an absence of many demographic, geographic and social drivers.

As you can see, cyclical hot spots are probably the easiest to identify early on because they are related to the real estate cycle as well as relying on an absence of drivers rather than a combination of them.

	NUMBER OF DRIVERS		WHICH CATEGORY OF DRIVERS				
	Early	Later	Early			Later	
			Demographic	Geographic	Social	Economic	Real Estate Market
Possible	5+	–	Any	Any	Any	–	–
Likely	7+	–	Any	Any	Any	–	–
Emerging	10+	3+	Any	Any	Any	Any	Any
Existing	10+	5+	Any	Any	Any	Any	Any
Cyclical	–	3+	–	–	–	Any	Any

Where can you source data and information on the hot spot drivers for your location?

1. Realtors/Real Estate Agents – Get as many realtors as possible to provide you with a list of real estate sales in the location from the preceding six to twelve months (or see mapping websites below). Then drive past those properties for a kerbside view of what has been selling in the location and for how much. That should give you a good indication of values in the location.

2. Internet – The Internet can assist you with gathering much historic information about the location you are assessing.

- Real estate agent websites.
- Real estate statistics websites. These are particularly useful for data on economic and real estate market hot spot drivers.
- News-based websites. Gather general information about the location by reading news-based websites for that location. Often the media will produce news stories relating to upcoming real estate developments or proposed new or improved public amenities in the location.
- Tellmethetime.com website. This is my own website dedicated to recording the progress of property cycles throughout the developed world.
- The local governing council or body for that region is also likely to have a website which contains information about proposals for upcoming new or improved public amenities in the area or planned infrastructure projects.
- Government statistics website.
- Police website for crime information.
- Mapping websites. Recently available mapping technology is revolutionising the global real estate industry by offering an improved level of availability of real estate market data. This improvement is enhancing the transparency of real estate market information.

3. Local knowledge – Driving around the location, visiting cafés, etc. is useful for observing social hot spot drivers in particular.

Hot spot driver contradictions

Hot spot drivers indicate the likelihood of a hot spot occurring, but when considering the drivers, you will also need to understand the contradictions. For example, one of the hot spot drivers is the rezoning of a location to allow for high-intensification with more dwellings permitted per site. The rezoning of a location improves real estate values when the economic value of the land will increase as a result of such rezoning. This rezoning could mean that where once just one dwelling stood there may now be the ability to build twelve dwellings. The contradiction arrives when values start increasing *before* such rezoning is formally approved. Some speculators will buy into the location on the hope that such a rezoning will occur, when in fact it may not. The local government body may decide not to proceed with the rezoning or may encounter resistance which precludes it from rezoning. So even when a suburb or location is increasing in value that does not in itself mean a suburb or location will continue to be a hot spot.

Another example of a hot spot driver contradiction is when rental demand is declining but real estate values are still increasing. Typically, you can expect values to fall when rental demand declines because rents underpin values to a certain degree, in particular the value of real estate to an investor.

You also need to consider other factors that could be driving up demand for real estate in a location. Perhaps more owner-occupiers are buying into the location and they typically do not consider the potential rental return of the property when assessing the price they are prepared to pay for it.

Some locations permanently demonstrate some of the hot spot drivers; for example, a waterfront suburb is always a waterfront location, but of course there are certain times during the real estate cycle when the premium for waterfront real estate reaches a cyclical peak.

Chapter Summary

▶ Hot spots emerge in a location when the supply of real estate is limited and demand for it is high and cold spots emerge when the demand for real estate is low and the supply of real estate is plentiful.

▶ The emergence of a hot spot typically occurs rapidly. However, a hot spot can sometimes be the result of slow and seemingly insignificant changes which incrementally bring about the perfect environment for exponential and rapid change.

▶ Some common drivers of demand, which I call hot spot drivers, typically result in a sharp increase in real estate values. It is more likely that several hot spot drivers will collectively be responsible for creating a hot spot than any single hot spot driver.

▶ The Internet offers easy access to much of the data, information and local news you need to assess locations for hot spots.

▶ Be aware there are usually some contradictions to take into account when assessing real estate hot spot drivers.

4

CHAPTER

How to Identify Hot Spots and Cold Spots

▶ Observation and common sense
▶ The game fishing syndrome
▶ Dangers to watch out for
▶ The herd mentality
▶ The bigger fool theory
▶ Are new developments fields of capital growth gold or fields of fool's gold?
▶ Different types of fields

Observation and common sense

You will need to be observant and use your common sense to find out as much as you can about the geographic, demographic, social, economic and real estate market factors impacting on a location, to be able to identify a real estate hot spot before it actually emerges as one. You will also be able to identify cold spots from this information. The 21st century has seen consumers demanding increased transparency of real estate data and fortunately the Internet can offer a great platform to assess such information.

I have categorised the typical hot spot drivers into a checklist in the previous chapter to simplify their identification. The more of these drivers that are evident in a location, the more likely it is that the location will become a real estate hot spot.

To identify a cold spot location is relatively easy because the location will have a noticeable absence of many hot spot drivers!

Let's consider the importance of common sense and observation in helping you identify hot spots and cold spots. Observation is the number one requirement for becoming a real estate hot spot or cold spot spotter!

I say common sense is required because some of the drivers that can help identify a hot spot just make common sense. For example, if rents in a suburb or location are rising rapidly then it is reasonable to believe that real estate values in that location will also rise in due course. This makes common sense because the higher return on investment available from the higher rents will increase the value of real estate to an investor. Of course, the opposite also applies, so in the event of reducing rents we can expect values to subsequently decline, creating the environment for a potential cold spot.

While we know that rents will increase rapidly as a result of accommodation shortages, it is important to understand why that shortage is occurring. Is it because of some reason that can cause a hot spot to emerge or is it because of some other reason that will not necessarily result in the location becoming a hot spot?

For example, an influx of people attracted by a buoyant economy or a new large employer is likely to result in the location becoming a hot spot. But if the influx of people to the location is a result of a short-term but high-profile sports event, for example, which is attracting strong short-term accommodation demand, then it is unlikely to become a hot spot with sustainable value growth.

This is why you need to be observant. You will need to observe not only what is happening in the location but also why those changes are occurring. Initially the hard work is seeking out as much unbiased information as possible for the locations that you think may become hot spots. Once you have access to the right information it becomes relatively easy to identify real estate hot spots or cold spots.

Seeking out hot spots takes much patience and lots of research that may only result in you deciding *not* to buy there because the location is unlikely to become a hot spot. The patience you need reminds me of the patience you sometimes need when game fishing.

The game fishing syndrome

I had been on a game fishing charter for so many hours that it seemed like days on end. All I could hear was the droning of the boat while we towed plastic around the ocean for miles and miles and miles with no game fish to be seen. Suddenly there was a strike, a 'whizzing' and a hive of activity on the boat. Finally, a fish had struck one of the lures. 'Clear the deck!' yelled the skipper. To clear the deck we had to reel in all of the other fishing rods and move the beer bottles out of the way. Then in the distance the bill of a marlin flew out of the water and then the marlin itself, briefly lighting up in a stream of sunlight. Then even though we couldn't see it we could hear the 'whizzing' of the fishing line as the fish dived deep. It slowed almost to a stop and then took off again and all I could hear was the screaming line and the havoc and panic on the deck. After fifteen minutes or so of slowly winding the fish closer to the boat suddenly I saw deep purple and green colours emerging from the water, stunning colour combinations and a large almost pure black eye. Then just as quickly as it had arrived the fish was tagged and released back into the deep blue and we all celebrated before everything became quiet again. All I could hear was the droning of the boat while we towed plastic around the ocean for miles and miles and miles.

The moral of the game fishing syndrome is that most of the action happens in a relatively short space of time. Chasing hot spots will be much like game fishing with a lot of time spent seeking out and weighing up the information you need to assess the likelihood of a hot spot's emergence. In fact, most of your time will probably be spent 'towing plastic lures around the sea' but that's what's usually needed to achieve a positive result whether you are fishing for marlin or seeking out hot spots.

Dangers to watch out for

Some dangers exist when buying into hot spots, because there can be factors which may prove a location's downfall or may have an impact on your financial return.

Be wary of the following factors which can negatively impact on locations:

Rapidly mobile tenants – For example, international students who can easily find more cost-effective, better-quality and/or convenient locations.

High maintenance properties or management expenses deflating returns – Your initial yield may be high but if the property has high ongoing maintenance and/or costs associated with ownership then your return on investment after expenses may be very low or even negative.

Over-regulation – Beware of seeking hot spots in countries with heavy regulations such as restrictions on foreign ownership, or with a restrictive lending policy, restrictive real estate policy or lack of structure for legal title to be granted for land.

Tax policy – Some countries' tax policies will make speculative real estate trading uneconomic and/or with limited write-offs allowable against income, a capital gains tax, federal taxes, etc.

Land claims – Typically land claims are made by indigenous peoples with a potential claim to ancestral land rights or ownership of the land of their forebears. Land claims can also be made by the local government body 'reclaiming' land for roading or other purposes.

High acquisition costs – The costs involved with acquiring real estate vary from country to country, but expect to pay anywhere between 5 per cent and 15 per cent of the purchase price. Obviously if you are trading properties this high acquisition cost can impact negatively on your profit margin.

An article in *The Economist* magazine, 29 May 2003, entitled 'Design Flaws' indicated the following estimated combined costs of buying and selling property.

COUNTRY	% COST OF TOTAL PURCHASE PRICE
Belgium	18%
France	15%
Italy	14%
Spain	13%
USA	12%
Germany	10%

COUNTRY	% COST OF TOTAL PURCHASE PRICE
Australia	8%
Ireland	6%
Japan	5%
Britain	4%

[New Zealand   3%]

The herd mentality

The herd mentality is the term given to a group's behaviour when many people's actions are the same. Real estate investors often employ similar investment strategies at the same time. For example, when a location offers high yields compared with comparable locations nearby, many investors will start investing in real estate in that location.

Typically, when a herd of real estate investors is investing heavily in one location that location will ultimately suffer a reduction in demand. Frequently this is because, sooner or later, the herd will find somewhere that higher returns can be achieved with less risk. Hence investors will move as a herd and therefore reduce demand.

Be wary of the herd mentality; just because everyone else thinks a location is a great investment, doesn't mean it's necessarily true or will become true.

The bigger fool theory

The bigger fool theory is when you think if I am prepared to pay this much for this property then someone else must be prepared to pay the same or more for it.

Many property buyers rely on the sales prices of similar properties to justify how much a property may be worth but this measure can be flawed. That measure will not account well in a falling market, because sales are historic and just because a comparable property next door sold for a certain amount that doesn't mean that your property will also sell for the same amount or more. This is what I refer to as the 'bigger fool theory'.

So don't just rely on the sale prices of similar properties in the area, but look also for clues from the hot spot drivers to confirm that the area may be a hot spot.

Are new developments fields of capital growth gold or fields of fool's gold?

New developments can range from a single additional dwelling being added to a site which already has a dwelling on it to 10,000 or more new dwellings on 10,000 or more new sites, for example, a subdivision.

Unfortunately, all too often real estate developers will promote their latest development as a chance to achieve fantastic capital growth. Some of the marketing implies that *their development* is a 'field' of capital growth gold in which you can stake your claim by purchasing a property, and then just sit back and harvest the capital growth as values in the area continue to rise. They will often highlight all of the positive influences on the area their development is located in and use them to justify ever-increasing demand for occupants and, therefore, ever-increasing real estate values. While in some cases this may be true, it is hard for potential purchasers to distinguish between those developments that genuinely are poised for capital growth and those developments which are merely being manipulated and marketed to achieve a sale by a developer with little, if any, regard for the future of real estate values in the area.

Sometimes these apparent fields of capital growth gold will actually self-preclude capital growth within the location. This occurs when there is too much supply or potential supply of properties in the area, causing an imbalance between supply and demand.

For example, an area that has previously had no housing on it, perhaps it was farmland or fields, which are now earmarked for new development, can evidence an imbalance between supply and demand. The development could have the capacity for 10,000 dwellings to be built, but there may only be enough people seeking to live in the area in the next year for 1000 dwellings.

In this case the laws of supply and demand should determine that real estate values in that area would remain 'soft' because of the excess supply of potential properties, i.e. the ability to build 10,000 when demand only exists for 1000, should to some degree preclude values from rising.

However, such an imbalance can be manipulated by a developer because they can simply maintain the 'scarcity factor' by restricting the supply of new properties available for sale at any one time. For example, if demand exists for 1000 dwellings in the next year then a developer will not build 10,000 dwellings as they know they will not be able to sell most of them and the values of their remaining 9000 houses would fall because the level of supply would far outweigh the level of demand.

So a developer will not complete all 10,000 properties at once but will 'stage' the development by only releasing a limited number of dwellings for sale at any one time. This ensures they control the volume being released to the market to maintain the 'scarcity factor' and, therefore, ever-increasing sale prices.

Of course, locations where lots of developers are building all at once are unlikely to offer the developers the same opportunity to manipulate the level of supply. This is because if one developer doesn't supply enough properties for sale, the buyers will simply purchase a property from another developer.

So fields can sometimes offer the opportunity for capital growth (i.e. when developers can control the level of supply) but sometimes offer the perfect environment for values to decline (i.e. when developers have little control over the level of supply).

The real estate cycle can also have a significant impact on fields locations. Fields are often developed near the end of a real estate boom as the volume of developers reaches a cyclical peak. However, fields developments usually have a long lead-in time before the development commences and often developers will be caught short when the boom ends and the slump begins. Early in the slump the demand for real estate reduces so it becomes harder for developers to secure sales of developed real estate in the field.

While fields locations can sometimes offer good capital growth prospects, be aware that if the properties are priced too high by the developers in the first place then values may not increase and the developers may start discounting prices to make sales. In this event values may in fact decline. So you still need to do your research on local real estate values to make sure the property you buy is not overpriced in the first place.

How can you tell which new development 'field' is poised to be a hot spot or which one is poised to be a cold spot? The good news is you can learn the answer, but first you need to understand the variations or types of fields that exist.

Different types of fields

The various types of fields locations are defined below and described by colours such as green fields, brown fields, blue fields and clear fields. There are also new fields.

A green field is an area of significant land that is being built upon for the first time. Green is an appropriate colour because typically the fields are, or were, green.

A brown field is land that was formerly an industrial area and which is now being redeveloped for housing. Brown is an appropriate colour to describe what is usually a muddy or dusty site.

A blue field is an area developed over water (for example, reclaimed land) and a clear field is any area which is built in the sky (for example, a multi-storey apartment).

A new field is the term for a huge development across a large but still confined geographic area.

Let's consider which of these fields, if any, may truly be fields of capital growth gold.

The green field syndrome

The green field syndrome occurs when a new dwelling development is undertaken on a large scale on formerly undeveloped land. A large scale is exactly that . . . LARGE. For example, a development of just ten or even twenty new houses in itself will not result in the green field syndrome. However, a new development of a sizable scale such as a completely new suburb with the potential for hundreds of dwellings or more is a green field.

Usually in green field areas properties will initially increase significantly in value, even before any properties have been built. This is due to the demand generated by the developers through their marketing and promotion of the field as a desirable place to live. Of course, if the developer gives the properties a relatively high price initially (compared with surrounding locations), then value growth is likely to be suppressed and may even decrease in the short to medium term. Sometimes, though, developers will price the properties very competitively to achieve an early and strong level of interest from potential purchasers. This enables the developer to secure pre-sales or off-the-plan sales (i.e. sale of properties before they are constructed).

However, as developers continue to build more and more properties the demand eventually becomes saturated by an oversupply of buildings. This will result in some developers starting to suffer financial pressure from not being able to sell enough of their newly built properties and from the holding costs of any other vacant land they have purchased initially with the intention of developing. Some of the developers' properties will be sold at a discount to secure cash flow for the developer, therefore suppressing any further value growth of similar properties in the location. Bare lots will remain undeveloped due to the lack of demand and it will be cheaper to buy existing properties than to build a new one. Most likely this will put some downward pressure on the values of all real estate in the location. This pressure on values is likely to have the biggest impact on those who purchased properties in the green field after many new properties have already been constructed. I call these purchasers the 'secondary buyers'.

Therefore, the secondary buyers in the green field location may find they have paid too much for their properties as the supply and demand balance is tipped more in favour of supply. There are more properties available for purchase than there are buyers to purchase them.

In this case properties in the green field will be unlikely to experience much, if any, capital growth until demand for real estate in the location again exceeds the supply of properties for sale.

Sooner or later developers will oversupply the market again, saturating the demand. Once the amount of suitable land available to build upon in the green field becomes exhausted, values will become more stable and then experience more traditional capital growth in line with capital growth rates of the surrounding locations.

The green field syndrome will only abate once all land in the green field has been developed.

Green field stages

Green field developments traditionally experience the following stages:

▶ Early stage of development: demand exceeds supply
▶ Middle stage of development: supply exceeds demand
▶ Late stage of development: demand matches or exceeds supply.

You will note in the simulated graph on the following page of the typical green field syndrome that values increase rapidly in the early stage of a green field being developed. Values then increase even further in the initial period of the middle stage, but the effect of developers oversupplying the market results in a subsequent fall in values. Values are likely to fall back to a level experienced in the early stage of the green field development but will still remain higher than they were initially.

Then values will plateau before demand again exceeds the level of supply of available properties, therefore setting the scene for values to increase again.

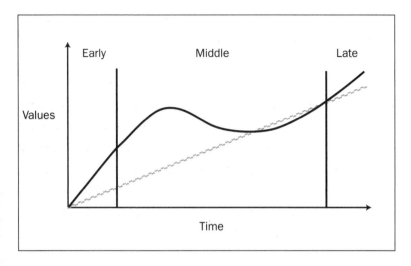

Graph 4.1

So if you want to capitalise on a green field location buy at the beginning of the early phase of the location's development, when demand far exceeds the level of supply.

Clear fields

Clear fields are dwellings built in the sky and are often in the CBD of large cities. In the traditional progression of the business cycle, in times of economic downturns many businesses suffer from contraction or failure and this results in many commercial properties becoming vacant. Every city is reliant on a high level of occupants to financially prosper and to be able to afford to upgrade public amenities. So a slump in business, resulting in a high vacancy rate, can sometimes cause local authorities to review and then amend development policy to support the construction of apartments in large numbers. This is one way to ensure that more people actually occupy the CBD, thus increasing occupancy rates while securing cash flow for the local authorities in the form of increased taxes and rates for local services. This policy amendment also achieves the economies of scale required for it to become economic for developers to purchase tracts of land to develop into new apartments.

The ultimate effect of the clear field syndrome is that too many apartments are likely to be constructed, resulting in an oversupply similar to that often experienced by green fields. A period of oversupply is inevitable if the number of apartments being built is larger than the level of demand for them. As developers build more and more properties the demand becomes satisfied and consequently the market becomes oversupplied. Some developers' stock will then be sold at discounted prices in a 'forced' sale situation. Usually when a significant case of oversupply is becoming evident, the local governing authority will revisit its development policy and typically will tighten up the regulations to stem the flow of surplus apartments being constructed. Alternatively, they will not adjust their regulations but will simply let the oversupply itself cause a correction in values.

New fields

Sometimes new areas are developed on a very large scale. These are usually a combination of green fields, clear fields, blue fields and sometimes even brown fields. A good example right now is Dubai where they are building on land that was formerly uninhabitable desert 'all made possible by desalination technology that has turned the salt waters of the Persian Gulf into an inexhaustible reservoir'. They are also building in the sky and over water.

These excerpts are from Ambrose Evans-Pritchard in *The New Zealand Herald*, 13 May 2006.

The Persian Gulf region is experiencing development on a

massive scale. So large that it involves a trillion US dollars of investment with over half of that being spent on construction, hotels and real estate.

What is happening in the Persian Gulf region right now includes:

- Smelting and industrial hub US$130 billion
- Airport capacity for 200 million passengers
- New city for 150,000 people and 29 hotels US$28 billion
- Silk City housing 700,000 people
- Nine months to build a 50-storey apartment block
- Pearl Islands Complex
- Safe haven for Iranians seeking a bolthole
- Population 36 million
- Concern that too many properties could be being built without anyone to occupy them
- Few if any barriers to foreign real estate ownership
- Media, showbiz, sporting and money centrepoint
- Biggest shopping mall in the world
- 'Desert Disney' US$20 billion
- Economy benefiting from oil prices over US$70/barrel
- Twenty per cent of all the world's high tower cranes are working in the Persian Gulf.

'Dubai is like the city states of Venice and Genoa in the middle ages, dynamic out of all proportion to the size of its population', said Maurice Flanagan, the co-founder of Emirates Airline, itself now conquering global aviation.

In my opinion, Dubai will continue to evidence good capital growth for a few more years yet, maybe longer, and especially while underpinned by strong oil prices. Inevitably a day of reckoning will arrive if values continue to boom, and some people are bound to lose money on real estate investments when the unavoidable oversupply becomes apparent. At that time many properties will be vacant for long periods.

So in summary of the new fields I think they have 'legs' (that is, they can deliver capital growth for many years) but are likely to eventually be subject to volatility in values as the balance between demand and supply is disturbed.

Green, Clear and New Fields Secrets

Buy early in green, clear and new field areas. Buy before many properties have been developed and when the demand is much stronger than the ability for the market to supply.

Don't buy in the secondary stage of the development of the area unless you have a long-term view. If you don't buy early, consider buying if (or when) the field becomes oversupplied with properties, but wait for values to experience significant negative capital growth first.

Brown fields

This is the term used to describe developments on former commercial or industrial land. Brown fields are developed because typically their former or current use is no longer economic or has been long abandoned. I include quarries, swamps or wasteland areas which are 'cleaned up' and developed in the definition of brown fields.

Sometimes the site is cleaned up and soil is treated or removed altogether. New roads, landscaping and trees arrive quickly and suddenly the brown field area becomes a desirable trendy part of town. A good example of a brown field is the austral brick works at Eastwood in Australia which is being converted into a development of homes for 500 people. The location of brown fields is often superior to green fields as the surrounding area has usually already been developed and upgraded over many years. Often the desirability of brown fields is enhanced by their proximity to shopping precincts, good schools, good transport and established local communities. These features combined with the actual new dwellings can make some brown field areas much more desirable than alternative new dwelling locations.

The Sydney Morning Herald, Monday 21 November 2005
For the next three years trucks will collect dirt from work sites across the city and travel to the brick works. They will work almost non-stop to fill in an old Shale quarry, an enormous 2 million cubic metre hole that developers hope to transform into a groovy urban village. The convoys will cart the rubble . . . up to 150 truck trips a day, six days a week in a routine spanning nearly 40 months . . .

Property groups are finding the end products are being embraced by a new breed of owner, many of whom want the polished finish of a new development but also the community vibe of an established suburb . . . The former site of the brick works will house more than 500 residents in more than 260 apartments and other dwellings and the development includes a heritage-style village nestled between old brick kilns and chimneys and is located just a kilometre from one of the city's better train stations.

There are examples of brown field areas in most cities and having opportunity to be one of the first purchasers is usually a good way of securing capital growth.

Blue fields

I give the term blue fields to land that is reclaimed or created on top of water. Good examples of blue fields areas are seen in many large seaside cities where parts of the central business district have been constructed on top of landfill which was used to 'extend' the land out over the water. Other good examples of blue fields areas are buildings constructed on top of existing wharves.

Blue fields can sometimes suffer the same effects as green fields; however, typically, blue fields are much smaller developments, therefore the level of demand for blue field real estate will often exceed the supply. Thus in blue fields it's not necessarily as dangerous to purchase real estate in the secondary stage of development.

Brown and Blue Fields Secrets

Buy early in the brown and blue fields. Buy before many properties have been developed and when the demand is much stronger than the ability for the market to supply.

Brown and blue fields typically don't become oversupplied because they are usually strictly limited in their level of supply of property unlike green, clear and new fields, which have a large potential for additional supply.

Chapter Summary

▶ In order to identify a location as a real estate hot spot before it actually emerges as one, you need to use your common sense, be observant and find out as much as you can about the economic, geographic, demographic and social factors impacting on the area. You will also need to find recent real estate market data for the area.

▶ If properties are initially priced too high by developers then values may not increase and the developers may start discounting prices to make sales. In this event values may in fact decline. So you still need to do your research on local real estate values to make sure the property you buy is not overpriced.

▶ Become informed about the factors that can impact negatively on hot spots.

▶ Be wary of the herd mentality. Just because everyone else thinks a property is a good buy, doesn't mean it is.

▶ Don't rely solely on property sales data to establish the value of a property, because sales are historic.

▶ Fields can sometimes offer the opportunity for capital growth (i.e. when developers can control the level of supply), but they can also create the perfect environment for values to decline (i.e. when developers have little control over the level of supply).

5

Hot Spot Goal Setting

- ▶ Establish your goals and set your rules
- ▶ Help to establish your real estate hot spots goals
- ▶ Recycled leveraging
- ▶ Real estate hot spots goal work sheet
- ▶ Constantly review your progress
- ▶ Real estate hot spots goal monitoring template
- ▶ Do your homework

Establish your goals and set your rules

In Chapter 1, I explained how I achieved an annual return of over 130 per cent per annum compounding for four years by investing in hot spots. Before I embarked on my quest to multiply my initial small investment I set myself a five-year goal.

My goal was to invest in real estate that achieved at least a 10 per cent per annum capital growth rate for five years and to increase my initial investment of $20,000 to at least $300,000. I intended to borrow 90 per cent of the purchase price of the first property I bought so I intended to purchase a property for around $200,000 with a mortgage of $180,000. After one year and 10 per cent capital growth this property should be worth at least $220,000 and at that point I could benefit from leveraging off its increased value. I would use this increased value to then support a 100 per cent mortgage to fund a second property. If each year I only bought one property with a 90 per cent mortgage I calculated that by year five with five properties owned I could turn my original $20,000 into more than $300,000.

Even with my limited amount of knowledge and 'market intelligence' on the topic of hot spots at that time I was able to pinpoint a location and buy a property which increased by a whopping 26 per cent in the first year I owned it, establishing my ability to further multiply my initial $20,000 investment!

You might think I got lucky but I make my own luck by making well-researched and informed decisions. In year two I achieved a 25 per cent average capital growth rate.

But in year three I only achieved a 'low' 10 per cent average capital growth rate. In part this 'low' capital growth rate was caused by an overall slowing of the real estate market as a result of the misperception that a real estate crash was inevitable. But there were no statistical analyses or facts to back up this perception.

At that time my own in-depth analysis of real estate cycles clearly indicated there was *no* crash coming and I announced that to the media. But the media were generally not interested in publishing my view probably because it was not as sensational as the 'crash message'. My analysis was proven correct in time – the market fundamentals that I had identified as reasons there would *not* be a crash had prevailed.

Ironically the misperception of a coming crash worked in my favour. I could see opportunities in the market which simply hadn't existed the year before, and I capitalised on them. This confirmed that even hot spots are not immune to being impacted by factors you are not expecting that can negatively influence the entire real estate market. The good news was that in spite of a softer market I still achieved a 10 per cent capital growth rate because I had invested in cyclical hot spot locations.

In year four I achieved another 17 per cent growth in the values of the properties I had funded entirely from my initial $20,000 investment.

My quest was a resounding success and after just four years I had multiplied my initial investment of just $20,000 into more than $600,000! In hindsight my goal was far too conservative, but in 2001 I didn't understand the true power of what my quest would teach me.

You too will need to set some goals and guidelines, or rules, which you will need to abide by to assist with your safe decision-making.

Your rules give you a platform you can use to balance your risk with your opportunity to create profits. Even still, you may find there are times when your decision-making ends in a poor result – that is in part the nature of investing in real estate. It can be a high-risk business with potential high profitability but also the potential for real and significant financial losses.

Occasionally even when you think you can't go wrong, you can and you do. Unfortunately, sometimes events occur that are completely out of your control, or even your ability to foresee their occurrence, which can have a dramatic negative effect on the value of real estate. However, you can reduce your risk significantly if you establish some clear goals (of exactly what it is you are attempting to achieve) at the outset and then follow your own set of rules to help you achieve those goals with a limited amount of risk. There will be occasions when you'll be tempted for one reason or another to break your own rules – be very cautious about doing so.

When you are tempted to break your own rules you will need to:
1. Remind yourself that you set those rules for a specific and very valid reason which was to balance your acceptable level of risk with your desired level of return.
2. Adjust your rules to reflect your willingness to accept a higher level of risk, but then you should also adjust your rules to achieve a higher level of return. This higher level of return should reflect the higher level of risk you are now prepared to accept.

Of course, your main goal may simply be to buy a property to live in and secondary be to achieve some wealth creation. Or you may aspire to become the next Donald Trump through real estate investment! Either way, you would be wise to clarify your goals and support them with some rules.

Help to establish your real estate hot spots goals

It is common knowledge that goals must contain certain elements to be achieved. I use the **SMARTER** acronym to define these elements.

Specific   A vague goal will end in a vague result. Be specific.

Measurable   You cannot manage what you cannot measure.

Achievable   Make sure your goal is achievable within the time-frame you need to achieve it.

Realistic   Make sure your goal is realistic based on your resources, knowledge and skills.

Time bound   Put a timeframe on your goal so it has an end.

Exit strategy Add how you will know when and how to 'exit' the goal (i.e. access your profits).

Review   Goals don't have to be set in concrete and should be regularly reviewed in light of new information, experience and knowledge. Make sure the goal remains appropriate to your ever-changing needs.

The level of risk you are prepared to take and the potential return you are attempting to achieve should determine whether you take a passive or aggressive stance to investing in hot spots. Your passive or aggressive stance gives some indication of the types of hot spots you should invest in.

In Chapter 1, I detailed which hot spots are suitable for passive or aggressive investing (based on their respective levels of risk and return) as follows:

Conservative: Emerging, cyclical
Neutral: Existing
Aggressive: Possible, likely

Example 1: A passive goal for profiting from real estate hot spots:

I intend to purchase real estate in real estate hot spots so I can achieve a minimum 15 per cent return per annum (on my initial investment) compounding over the next five years.

Here is an example of some rules for passively profiting from real estate hot spots:

1. Need to achieve a 15 per cent per annum compounding return on my investment
2. Only to be achieved by purchasing in an emerging or cyclical hot spot
3. Only buy in *established* suburbs or locations, i.e. no *fields* purchases
4. The 'exit' strategy: I will use a stop loss of 5 per cent (i.e. if any owned property falls in value by 5 per cent below my purchase price then I will sell that property). Alternatively, I will sell when values have increased by 10 per cent (unless the hot spot drivers indicate the location will continue to be a hot spot).

The example rules above minimise the level of risk by only buying in emerging or cyclical hot spots in established suburbs. Risk is also minimised by excluding any 'fields' purchases. The use of a stop loss system is again to minimise risk, but it can be difficult to 'cap' a loss at 5 per cent because values can drop further than that very quickly. For example, you may only realise that values are declining when a comparable property to yours sells for 10 per cent less than you paid for your property. That is one of the downsides of the real estate investing stop loss system. You cannot easily establish a stop loss system that will trigger a sale once values decline to a certain level. Thus, values may have fallen much further than you realised, or were prepared to sell at, before you are even aware they have fallen. For a real estate stop loss system to be of much use to you, you will need to very closely monitor real estate value trends on an ongoing basis. The exit strategy also has a timeframe, although, due to the low-risk nature of these rules, that timeframe is dependent on value increases being achieved. In other words, if values don't increase to the required level, it may pay to retain the property until values do. Of course, we know that time has a diminishing effect on your real estate return too so you need to consider whether or not you should retain the property or sell it.

So, back to our example. If you started with $40,000 cash and bought a property with no mortgage then after five years if you have achieved a 15 per cent return per annum compounding growth rate, your initial $40,000 would turn into more than $80,000. Of course, to expect real estate values to increase by 15 per cent per annum consistently for five years may not be that realistic. However, we don't need real estate values to increase by 15 per cent per annum because we can achieve leverage from borrowing relatively high levels of funds against real estate assets. In fact, if you borrowed 80 per cent of the value of a property upon purchase then real estate values would only have to increase by 10 per cent per annum for us to achieve a compounding growth rate of more than 30 per cent on our initial investment. This is the result of leverage.

Leverage is one of the significant benefits of investing in real estate over other asset classes such as shares, mutual funds or managed funds. Real estate gives you access to high leverage combined with the ability to achieve compounding returns. This high leverage is possible because financial institutions are aware that one of the basic human needs is for housing, so financial institutions are generally prepared to lend a relatively higher percentage of the value of real estate than they would lend on other asset classes.

Let's consider a simple example of the compounding effects that real estate value increases can have on your investment:

Starting cash (equity)	$ 40,000 – 20%
Borrowing from bank	$160,000 – 80%

AN INSIDER'S GUIDE TO REAL ESTATE HOT SPOTS

Purchase property for	$200,000 – 100%

Real estate values increase by 10% in year one:

Property value is now	$220,000
Borrowing from bank	$160,000 – 73%
Your equity	$ 60,000 – 27%

Your return for one year = $20,000 or 50% on your original $40,000 which is now $60,000

Real estate values increase by 10% in year two:

Property value is now	$242,000
Borrowing from bank	$160,000 – 66%
Your equity	$ 82,000 – 34%

Your return for one year = $22,000 or 36.67% on your $60,000

Real estate values increase by 10% in year three:

Property value is now	$266,200
Borrowing from bank	$160,000 – 60%
Your equity	$106,200 – 40%

Your return for one year = $24,200 or 29.51% on your $82,000

Real estate values increase by 10% in year four:

Property value is now	$292,820
Borrowing from bank	$160,000 – 54.5%
Your equity	$132,820 – 45.5%

Your return for one year = $26,620 or 25.07% on your $106,200

Real estate values increase by 10% in year five:

Property value is now	$322,102
Borrowing from bank	$160,000 – 49.5%
Your equity	$162,102 – 50.5%

Your return for one year = $29,282 or 22.05% on your $132,820

Your original $40,000 investment is now worth $162,102. That's more than four times your original investment in just five years and equates to a compounding per annum return of 32.30 per cent, even though properties only increased by 10 per cent per annum!

You may, however, have observed from the numbers above that each year you achieve a diminishing level of return. For example, in year one you achieve a 50 per cent return on your equity, but in year two you achieve a 36.67 per cent return and so on until in year five you only achieve a 22 per cent return.

This is because each year your percentage equity stake in the property is increasing as the value of the property increases. Therefore, you are achieving a reasonable but diminishing level of return on your original investment.

This example assumes you simply buy one property and hold it for five years. Of course, values will need to consistently increase by at least 7 per cent per annum to achieve the compounding return of over 30 per cent per annum.

Assumptions

It is assumed that any interest cost on debt used to purchase the property is serviced by cash flow generated from the rental property purchased. Available cash on sale of property excludes ownership costs, buying and selling costs, such as legal fees, taxes, etc.

Later in this chapter you will find a Real Estate Hot Spots Goal Monitoring Template. I have used this template to illustrate the effect of the above example.

	NOW	1 YEAR	2 YEARS	3 YEARS	4 YEARS	5 YEARS
Required % Capital Growth		10	10	10	10	10
Actual % Capital Growth						
Property Value	200,000	220,000	242,000	266,200	292,820	322,102
Actual Property Value	200,000					
Mortgage	160,000	160,000	160,000	160,000	160,000	160,000
Actual Mortgage	160,000					
Investment (Property Value – Mortgage)	40,000	60,000	82,000	106,200	132,820	162,102
Actual Equity or Cash (*Property Value – Mortgage*)	40,000					
Required Profit		20,000	22,000	24,200	26,620	29,282
Actual Profit						
Required % Return (*Required Profit as a % of Actual Equity or Cash in the Previous Year*)		50	37	30	25	22
Actual Return (*Actual Profit as a % of Actual Equity or Cash in the Previous Year*)						

HOT SPOT GOAL SETTING

AFTER 1 YEAR (ADD NEW FIGURES)	NOW	1 YEAR				5 YEARS
Required % Capital Growth		10	10	10	10	10
Actual % Capital Growth		10				
Property Value	200,000	220,000	242,000	266,200	292,820	322,102
Actual Property Value	200,000	220,000				
Mortgage	160,000	160,000	160,000	160,000	160,000	160,000
Actual Mortgage	160,000	160,000				
Investment (Property Value – Mortgage)	40,000	60,000	82,000	106,200	132,820	162,102
Actual Equity or Cash (Property Value – Mortgage)	40,000	60,000				
Required Profit		20,000	22,000	24,200	26,620	29,282
Actual Profit		20,000				
Required % Return (Required Profit as a % of Actual Equity or Cash in the Previous Year)		50	37	30	25	22
Actual Return (Actual Profit as a % of Actual Equity or Cash in the Previous Year)		50				

AFTER 2 YEARS (ADD NEW FIGURES)	NOW		2 YEARS			5 YEARS
Required % Capital Growth		10	10	10	10	10
Actual % Capital Growth		10	12			
Property Value	200,000	220,000	242,000	266,200	292,820	322,102
Actual Property Value	200,000	220,000	246,400			
Mortgage	160,000	160,000	160,000	160,000	160,000	160,000
Actual Mortgage	160,000	160,000	160,000			
Investment (Property Value – Mortgage)	40,000	60,000	82,000	106,200	132,820	162,102
Actual Equity or Cash (Property Value – Mortgage)	40,000	60,000	86,400			
Required Profit		20,000	22,000	24,200	26,620	29,282
Actual Profit		20,000	26,400			
Required % Return (Required Profit as a % of Actual Equity or Cash in the Previous Year)		50	37	30	25	22
Actual Return (Actual Profit as a % of Actual Equity or Cash in the Previous Year)		50	44			

HOT SPOT GOAL SETTING

AFTER 3 YEARS (ADD NEW FIGURES)	NOW			3 YEARS		5 YEARS
Required % Capital Growth		10	10	10	10	10
Actual % Capital Growth		10	12	10		
Property Value	200,000	220,000	242,000	266,200	292,820	322,102
Actual Property Value	200,000	220,000	246,400	271,040		
Mortgage	160,000	160,000	160,000	160,000	160,000	160,000
Actual Mortgage	160,000	160,000	160,000	160,000		
Investment (Property Value – Mortgage)	40,000	60,000	82,000	106,200	132,820	162,102
Actual Equity or Cash (Property Value – Mortgage)	40,000	60,000	86,400	111,040		
Required Profit		20,000	22,000	24,200	26,620	29,282
Actual Profit		20,000	26,400	24,640		
Required % Return (Required Profit as a % of Actual Equity or Cash in the Previous Year)		50	37	30	25	22
Actual % Return (Actual Profit as a % of Actual Equity or Cash in the Previous Year)		50	44	29		

AFTER 4 YEARS (ADD NEW FIGURES)	NOW				4 YEARS	5 YEARS
Required % Capital Growth		10	10	10	10	10
Actual % Capital Growth		10	12	10	8	
Property Value	200,000	220,000	242,000	266,200	292,820	322,102
Actual Property Value	200,000	220,000	246,400	271,040	292,723	
Mortgage	160,000	160,000	160,000	160,000	160,000	160,000
Actual Mortgage	160,000	160,000	160,000	160,000	160,000	
Investment (Property Value – Mortgage)	40,000	60,000	82,000	106,200	132,820	162,102
Actual Equity or Cash (Property Value – Mortgage)	40,000	60,000	86,400	111,040	132,723	
Required Profit		20,000	22,000	24,200	26,620	29,282
Actual Profit		20,000	26,400	24,640	21,683	
Required % Return (Required Profit as a % of Actual Equity or Cash in the Previous Year)		50	37	30	25	22
Actual Return (Actual Profit as a % of Actual Equity or Cash in the Previous Year)		50	44	29	20	

AFTER 5 YEARS (ADD NEW FIGURES)	NOW					5 YEARS
Required % Capital Growth		10	10	10	10	10
Actual % Capital Growth		10	12	10	8	10
Property Value	200,000	220,000	242,000	266,200	292,820	322,102
Actual Property Value	200,000	220,000	246,400	271,040	292,723	321,996
Mortgage	160,000	160,000	160,000	160,000	160,000	160,000
Actual Mortgage	160,000	160,000	160,000	160,000	160,000	160,000
Investment (Property Value – Mortgage)	40,000	60,000	82,000	106,200	132,820	162,102
Actual Equity or Cash (Property Value – Mortgage)	40,000	60,000	86,400	111,040	132,723	161,996
Required Profit		20,000	22,000	24,200	26,620	29,282
Actual Profit		20,000	26,400	24,640	21,683	29,272
Required % Return (Required Profit as a % of Actual Equity or Cash in the Previous Year)		50	37	30	25	22
Actual Return (Actual Profit as a % of Actual Equity or Cash in the Previous Year)		50	44	29	20	22

Recycled leveraging

If you are interested in achieving a non-diminishing return on your initial investment then you will need to be a bit smarter than just buying a property to hold for the medium term.

This is where recycled leveraging can help you.

If you are prepared to increase your level of risk (and you will using this strategy) then you can 'recycle' your original $40,000 each year by selling the property within twelve months. You then purchase in another real estate hot spot using your recycled funds as a full 20 per cent cash deposit and sell that property within twelve months, repeating this pattern for five years.

You will increase your risk because you will need to be able to consistently 'pick' hot spots and you would be investing more and more after each sale as you would have a higher dollar deposit than you had previously, allowing you to buy a more expensive property or even more than one property in a hot spot area. I refer to this concept as recycled leveraging.

If you are a more aggressive investor then recycled leveraging can turn an average capital growth rate into a spectacular return on your initial investment, especially if you are prepared to be disciplined enough to learn how to find and capitalise on real estate hot spots. On the other hand, recycled leveraging can quickly wipe out your entire net worth in just a few bad real estate deals. There is a significantly increased level of risk when adopting the recycled leveraging strategy.

Example 2: An aggressive goal for profiting from real estate hot spots

I intend to purchase property in real estate hot spots so I can achieve a minimum 50 per cent return per annum compounding over the next five years.

Here is an example of an appropriate set of rules for profiting from real estate hot spots:

1. Need to achieve a 50 per cent per annum compounding return on investment
2. To be achieved by purchasing in a possible or likely hot spot
3. To consider buying in *fields* locations (with appropriate timing)
4. The 'exit' strategy: I will use a stop loss of 10 per cent (i.e. if any owned property falls in value by 10 per cent below my purchase price then I will sell that property). Alternatively, I will sell when values increase by 20 per cent or within one year from purchase date, whichever occurs first (unless the hot spot drivers indicate the location will continue to be a hot spot).

Remember your risk is significantly increased by using an aggressive strategy such as recycled leveraging. Risk is also increased by being prepared to buy in any 'fields' locations. The use of a stop loss system is again to minimise risk but it can be difficult to 'cap' a loss because values can move very quickly.

Let's consider a simple example of recycled leveraging based on only achieving a 10 per cent increase in value (plus resale costs).

Your starting position:

Purchase property for	$200,000
Borrowing from bank	$160,000
Starting cash (equity)	$40,000

AN INSIDER'S GUIDE TO REAL ESTATE HOT SPOTS

Real estate values increase by 10% in year one:

Property value is now	$220,000
Borrowing from bank	$160,000
Your equity	$60,000

Your return = $20,000 or 50% on your original $40,000 which is now $60,000

Available cash on sale of property = $60,000

Your new 'starting' position in year two:

Purchase property for	$300,000
Borrowing from bank	$240,000 – 80%
Your equity	$60,000 – 20%

Real estate values increase by 10% in year two:

Property value is now	$330,000
Borrowing from bank	$240,000
Your equity	$90,000

Your return = $30,000 or 50% on your $60,000

Available cash on sale of property = $90,000

Your new 'starting' position in year three:

Purchase property for	$450,000
Borrowing from bank	$360,000 – 80%
Your equity	$90,000 – 20%

Real estate values increase by 10% in year three:

Property value is now	$495,000
Borrowing from bank	$360,000
Your equity	$135,000

Your return = $45,000 or 50% on your $90,000

Available cash on sale of property = $135,000

Your new 'starting' position in year four:

Purchase property for	$675,000
Borrowing from bank	$540,000 – 80%
Your equity	$135,000 – 20%

Real estate values increase by 10% in year four:

Property value is now	$742,500
Borrowing from bank	$540,000
Your equity	$202,500

Your return = $67,500 or 50% on your $135,000

Available cash on sale of property = $202,500

Your new 'starting' position in year five:

Purchase property for	$1,012,500
Borrowing from bank	$810,000 – 80%
Your equity	$202,500 – 20%

Real estate values increase by 10% in year five:

Property value is now	$1,113,750
Borrowing from bank	$ 810,000
Your equity	$ 303,750

Your return = $101,250 or 50% on your $202,500

Available cash on sale of property = $303,750

Recycled leveraging is a clear winner when it comes to a return on investment, if you are prepared to accept the higher level of risk that it brings. The power of recycled leveraging means even if you just achieve a 10 per cent capital growth rate per annum then you can effectively achieve an annual return of 50 per cent per annum compounding for five years.

You would achieve a net return on your initial $40,000 of over $260,000.

Recycled leveraging is only recommended for experienced real estate investors who understand real estate hot spots and can spot them consistently before it's too late. Even then recycled leveraging investors need to clearly understand that it can lead to wealth destruction.

Assumptions

▶ Any interest cost on debt used to purchase the property is serviced by cash flow generated from the rental property purchased.

▶ Available cash on sale of property excludes ownership costs, and buying and selling costs, such as legal fees, taxes, etc.

Real Estate Hot Spots Goal Worksheet

Timeframe (actual months or years): ....

By (insert actual date): ....

Input (insert actual initial investment): ....

Required output:

Annual percentage return per annum............................... %

Annual percentage return compounding........................... %

Rules

• I will only purchase real estate if I have sound reason to believe I can achieve ....% per annum capital growth and a compound per annum return of ....%.

• I will only purchase real estate in .... hot spots (i.e. either one or more of the types of hot spots such as an emerging hot spot, a likely hot spot or an existing hot spot).

• I will take a .... approach (i.e. passive or aggressive).

• I will use a stop loss of .... % (i.e. if any owned property falls in value by ....% then I will sell that property).

Constantly review your progress

Investing in real estate hot spots to create wealth will require you to closely monitor your progress towards your goal. This is easy to do if you have a suitable system to measure your progress.

Your system for measuring goals should be a simple framework to which you can apply your specific details and then measure your progress against. That way you can monitor whether you are on target to achieve your goal or not.

The specific items you will need to measure on an ongoing basis are:

1. Percentage of capital growth rate for the location
2. Current value of the property
3. Mortgage
4. Investment (your equity)
5. Profit in $
6. Profit in % return

On the following page is the template used for the example outlined earlier in this chapter. You can also use this template to record and measure your progress.

Real Estate Hot Spots Goal Monitoring Template

	NOW	1 YEAR	2 YEARS	3 YEARS	4 YEARS	5 YEARS
Required % Capital Growth						
Actual % Capital Growth						
Property Value						
Actual Property Value						
Mortgage						
Actual Mortgage						
Investment (Property Value – Mortgage)						
Actual Equity or Cash (Property Value – Mortgage)						
Required Profit						
Actual Profit						
Required % Return (Required Profit as a % of Actual Equity or Cash in the Previous Year)						
Actual Return (Actual Profit as a % of Actual Equity or Cash in the Previous Year)						

Do your homework

Get your funding organised

Before you can capitalise on real estate hot spots you must have access to suitable finance. Even if you have rather passive goals, you'll need to have finance arranged to assist with the purchase of real estate. If you have aggressive goals then you will need access to large amounts of finance. Seek out an excellent mortgage broker and make sure you don't rely on just one or two financiers to supply your funding to purchase properties. Financiers can and do adjust their lending policies when the real estate market suffers which makes it harder to qualify for finance, or worse still you may no longer qualify in terms of their new policy. This could result in you having to refinance at a time that may be difficult to do so. In the event you cannot refinance you may need to sell your properties at a time when financing them is difficult. This impacts negatively on the level of demand for real estate and subsequently property values can decline. Minimise your financing risk by using several different lenders so your entire real estate portfolio is not as vulnerable to changes in real estate lending policies.

Take action

Although you do need to do your homework, you don't need the equivalent of a tertiary qualification in real estate before you can actually make some decisions and take action. Many people will overanalyse and overeducate by learning everything there is to know about real estate; and then still do nothing. Remember, if you want what others want but aren't able to get, then you will have to do what others won't do. Gather adequate information – then make your decision and act on it!

Goal blockers

You can expect many potential obstacles to possibly block your path to achieving your goals. I call these obstacles goal blockers.

The risk factor

Yes it's true, you will increase your risk profile as a result of investing in real estate . . . but the rewards can be significant based on little cash input. Don't let the risk factor paralyse you with fear. Whatever risk profile you are comfortable with will pretty much determine how aggressive or passive your real estate investment activities are.

As a general rule of thumb, the higher your risk profile the more risk you can take, and, thus, the higher your risk and the potential rewards will be.

So how are you going to have a stress-free sleep when you owe the bank *hundreds of thousands* or even *millions* of dollars?

Easy, you just need to focus on the wealth you are generating rather than the amount of debt you owe the banks. It's the old analogy of whether you consider a cup to be half full or half empty . . . the abundance mentality versus the scarcity mentality.

I guess I am a bit immune to the size of the numbers because of my twenty years' finance and banking experience. I have been exposed to numbers that many people would struggle to comprehend so a few million seems like a smallish amount to me!

The most important number for you to focus on is the ultimate wealth being generated by your investments. Remember, as a property investor your cash flow is your lifeblood. Without it you may well suffer financial stress and losses.

With respect to the level of risk you should take, I suggest that if you are over fifty years old, it's probably not the time for you to be aggressive as it is wise to keep your investing risks low when nearing retirement. You should adopt a more conservative stance. If you are forty to fifty then you can probably afford to take a slightly aggressive or more neutral stance. If you are under forty then you can probably afford to take a much more aggressive stance but be aware your risk will be higher too.

The fear factor

It is still potentially frightening to borrow another million dollars or even another few hundred thousand dollars. Creating a buffer of available credit and/or cash can reduce your fear. An amount equivalent to three months' fixed financial commitments should be adequate to get you through most temporary financial difficulties.

Apart from creating a buffer, you can reduce your level of fear by educating yourself. Join your local real estate investors' organisation, attend real estate trade shows and expos and build your own network of relevant contacts so you can expand your knowledge base. The more knowledge you have the better equipped you will be to recognise real estate hot spots. You will need all the help you can get to research real estate issues, values, rentability, return on investment, etc. Read a wide variety of books on the topic, but don't take everything as gospel. The more you read the more you will learn to recognise the useful books from the 'bookcase fillers'.

The real estate investment sceptics

There will always be critics of real estate investment. Often they have some vested interest in convincing people not to invest in real estate or they just may naively think that it's too hard to make money from real estate.

You will also meet the dream stealers and, usually, these are people who have lost their own real estate dream often due to some rash emotional investment decision in the past. They may still be paying for their former folly and they will be only too pleased to warn you about the risks of real estate investment. Yes, there are risks but we know they can be minimised.

The other sceptics include the media who love to report from a sensational perspective. One day it can be a good time to buy real estate and the very next it may no longer be, according to new media headlines. Sometimes it seems the more headlines you read, the more confused you get about what the property market is doing.

And there are always the doomsday theorists who will tell you about the nightmare tenant scenario where the tenants stop paying the rent and when they vacate the property they leave it damaged and it costs thousands of dollars to repair. While this can occur, it is not an adequate reason to put you off investing in real estate.

The market factor

The market factor is a 'roller coaster', because we know it will be volatile at times, giving big lifts in cash flow and/or values, but there will also be times when the market will deliver big value decreases as well.

While generally the market factor is predictable there can be sudden temporary influencing factors which can introduce perceived turmoil.

Chapter Summary

▶ Establishing a clear goal can help you balance your level of risk with your proposed level of return.

▶ Investing in emerging or cyclical hot spots is wise if you have passive goals.

▶ Investing in possible or likely hot spots is wise if you have aggressive goals.

▶ Recycled leveraging involves an increased level of risk, but the potential return is high.

▶ Continuously monitor your progress towards your goals.

▶ Always have an exit strategy.

6

CHAPTER

Three Steps to Investing in Hot Spots

- ▶ Set your goal and do your research
- ▶ Get excellent professional advice
- ▶ Ascertain your starting position
- ▶ *Step One* Create or borrow an adequate cash deposit
- ▶ *Step Two* Create equity
- ▶ *Step Three* Sell or retain the property

Set your goal and do your research

If you have not yet read the concept of goal setting outlined in the previous chapter I strongly suggest you do so before investing in hot spots. Investing in hot spots without a clear goal will most likely result in future confusion when you are making buying and selling decisions. Without establishing a goal how can you measure and manage your progress towards it? How will you know whether or not to sell and take your profit or wait? If you haven't

139

yet read Chapter 5 please do so before following the steps in this chapter.

Equally important as setting your goal is doing research on the hot spot drivers for locations. So if you have not yet read Chapter 3 I suggest it is also critical you do so before beginning the steps in this chapter. You can further minimise your risks by seeking out excellent advisors, motivated vendors and adding value to the properties you purchase.

Get excellent professional advice

If you decide to act on any of the ideas in this book it would also pay to consider the following issues with the relevant professionals. Don't rely on the advice of a well-meaning neighbour or friend, instead seek out the best advisors you can to verify the facts. Don't be in a rush to appoint your advisors – meet with them to assess their knowledge about the matters that will affect you, such as ownership structures, legal requirements and taxation obligations, before appointing them to act for you. Ensure they have suitable experience dealing with clients who are regularly buying and selling real estate for profit.

The solution to your needs in each of the following topics will be dependent upon your financial circumstances, your acceptable degree of risk and your expected level of return from investing. You will need legal and accounting advisors locally, in the country you reside in for taxation purposes, and internationally, in each country you buy real estate in, if you intend to invest in countries other than that in which you reside. This will ensure you comply with each country's legal and taxation regulations.

1. **Legal and real estate ownership obligations:** see a lawyer specialising in real estate law.

2. **Taxation obligations and effectiveness of real estate ownership entities:** see an accountant and/or taxation lawyer.
3. **Appropriateness and pricing of funding:** see a financier who specialises in real estate investment funding.
4. **Return on investment:** see an accountant, financial planner and real estate investment consultant/mentor or coach.
5. **Risk profile:** see an estate planning lawyer, insurance advisor, accountant, financier and property investment consultant/ mentor or coach.
6. **Succession planning:** see an estate planning lawyer, accountant, and financial planner.
7. **Exit strategy:** see an estate planning lawyer, accountant, financial planner, real estate investment consultant/mentor or coach.
8. **Clearly defined position and goals:** see an estate planning lawyer, accountant, financial planner, real estate investment consultant/mentor or coach.

Ascertain your starting position

To capitalise on a real estate hot spot you will need access to adequate cash (or utilise equity you have access to in existing real estate). Normally (but not always) you need at least 10 per cent of the purchase price as a deposit and a financial institution will then lend you the balance of the property's purchase price.

You will either be starting from 'scratch' (i.e. no real estate now and no cash deposit) or already own some real estate or have adequate cash to use as a deposit.

If you are starting from scratch, as I did on my journey into real estate investment, then you will need to be very careful you don't overcommit yourself financially. I was 24 years old when I bought my first property and back then I had little money, but I did have a reasonable earning capacity as a bank employee.

How to start from scratch is an interesting proposition that warrants some analysis. Many people have told me they have no money and can't save enough to raise an adequate deposit and so don't qualify for a mortgage. I believe most people can achieve real estate ownership if they are seriously committed to doing whatever it takes to achieve that goal as outlined in step one below.

Three steps to creating wealth from real estate hot spots

Step One: Create or borrow an adequate cash deposit

If you have an adequate cash deposit then go to Step Two. If you have *no cash* to start with then all you need to do is convert your resources into either enough cash or enough cash flow to achieve your goal of raising adequate deposit funds.

Your resources will include:
- Time
- Assets
- Intellect
- Knowledge

You can use your resources to create:
- Cash
- Cash Flow
- Cash Flow-producing assets
- Skills

It is possible to start investing in real estate without any cash at all. However, you should not necessarily be in a desperate hurry to begin investing if you have no money, but you should be in a desperate hurry to learn as much as you can about real estate investment.

And the good news is that you can accumulate knowledge about real estate investing while you are aiming for your initial financial goal (of raising a deposit). Knowledge will position you to make wise decisions and capitalise on the best opportunities when you eventually do raise an adequate deposit.

Option 1: Saving a cash deposit

This can simply be achieved by regularly saving enough money to build up an adequate deposit to qualify for a mortgage. Unfortunately, this will take several years for most people (if not longer), especially if you are already paying rent for your current accommodation.

Option 2: Borrowing a cash deposit

A. If you do not own any property now but have adequate cash flow from your earning capacity then you may be able to raise some, or all, of your initial deposit through short-term borrowing (i.e. up to five years) on personal loans. But I must warn you that you do need a strong income and discipline to stick to a rigid budget and to be able to do this without becoming financially burdened.

This is exactly how I funded much of the deposit for my very first property purchase back in 1987. I could afford to borrow the deposit on short-term funding (personal loan and credit card) with the balance by way of a mortgage, but I did have to make some lifestyle sacrifices as a result of the extra financial commitment these short-term loans required. I could not afford to go away on holidays or go out for entertainment because my cash flow was committed in the main to my financial obligations. My holidays were spent working on improving the property by painting and gardening to hopefully increase its value so I could increase my mortgage borrowings to repay my short-term borrowings and, therefore, reduce the high pressure on my cash flow.

You may be lucky enough to be able to borrow from family and may even be able to achieve such a loan with no formal repayment schedule.

B. If you already own some real estate now then you may be able to raise adequate funds based on the value of your existing real estate to use as a deposit on your next property purchase. But you will still need to demonstrate adequate cash flow to support the raising of the deposit.

Irrespective of which of the above methods you use to raise your deposit, make sure you do not overcommit yourself financially as this could lead to your property being sold by a foreclosure or mortgagee sale situation.

Key questions to ask vendors

It's one thing to buy in a property hot spot and wait for property values to increase but it's entirely another to get a bargain price property at the same time.

When looking for a real estate bargain your best method is to seek out a highly motivated vendor – one who must sell their property. Typically they have little choice but to sell, often due to a marital break-up or business commitments, or they have little time to sell due to financial distress or some other reason. Highly motivated vendors are the most negotiable vendors.

But how will you find a highly motivated vendor? They usually won't freely admit they have no choice but to sell or that they have to sell quickly because they are under financial pressure!

If you could only ask the vendor of a property a few questions to find out how motivated they are to sell, what would those questions be?

You need to focus on what you are trying to achieve from these questions – they must help you buy a bargain price property. There are two very simple and effective questions which can give you a good indication of how motivated your vendor is likely to be. You should attempt to find the answers to at least these two questions.

Why is this property being sold?
It's only when you have some idea of why the owner is selling that you will be able to gauge whether they are likely to sell at a bargain price. If the vendor answers this question with 'no real reason' there is a good chance you have found a motivated vendor. I say this because in my many years of considering properties to purchase I have been told hundreds of times that the vendor has 'no real reason' for selling. Interestingly, I have never met anyone who has *sold* a property for 'no real reason'. The fact that the vendor is not willing to disclose the reason indicates that they do not want you to know it as this may give you the upper hand if negotiations begin. Thus, there is every likelihood they are highly motivated to sell.

How soon would you like to complete the sale and receive full payment?
If the vendor wants to complete the sale quickly there is more likelihood that they are a highly motivated vendor.

145

To make it a little easier to identify the keenest vendors, I have created the motivation scale.

The motivation scale

The motivation scale below indicates:

▶ **How motivated a vendor/seller may or may not be –**
Motivation ranges from slightly motivated to very motivated. Slightly motivated vendors will be in a situation of not needing to sell the property but they don't really want the property and don't really need the cash either. Perhaps a cash flow may appeal to them and this is where you can assist. For example, you could offer to buy the property if they lend you the funds to do so, by way of a mortgage on the property – this is commonly referred to as vendor financing. That way the vendor can secure a cash flow from you as you repay the mortgage, and you can secure ownership of the property.

▶ **Where to find motivated vendors –** Again this depends on their circumstances but sometimes you will find motivated vendors in the most unlikely of places. Realtors are an obvious source, but also the Internet, newspapers, real estate magazines, other investors that you know, local real estate managers who have a network of investors, mortgagee/foreclosure sales (usually advertised in local publications), trade deals (where you trade assets for other assets with maybe a part cash payment by either party, depending on the value of the assets concerned), and even driving around a neighbourhood can bring local knowledge and opportunity to the observant. Be curious about what is happening in the area.

▶ **What clues or words indicate how keen they are to sell –** This gives you some indication of whether you should focus more

MOTIVATION SCALE

Motivation of vendor/ seller	Circumstances	Where you may typically find them						Words that indicate the vendor's motivation	You should focus on	Negotiation tactics to use
		Realtors, newspapers, Internet, walk & talk	Other investors	Property manager	Mortgagee sale	Trade deals	Drive past			
Slightly motivated (Vendor has a lot of time)	Ageing	X	X	X				Vendor finance available, 2nd mortgage available	Terms	Long-term settlement or long-term vendor finance to enhance their cash flow
Don't want the property but don't need the cash						X		Long-term settlement, may accept trade		
Becoming more motivated (Vendor has some time)	Business opportunity	X	X	X				Cashing up, vacant, vendor has bought	Price & Terms	Quick settlement, cash offer
	Retiring	X	X	X				Vendor relocating, vendor going overseas		Remove their stress
Don't want the property but need the cash	Separation	X	X	X				Vendors parting ways, move in immediately		
	Tax issues	X	X	X				Employment transfer, needs work, do-up		
	Bought other property	X	X							
	Moving away	X	X							

MOTIVATION SCALE CONT'D

Motivation of vendor/seller	Circumstances	Where you may typically find them						Words that indicate the vendor's motivation	You should focus on	Negotiation tactics to use
		Realtors, newspapers, Internet, walk & talk	Other investors	Property manager	Mortgagee sale	Trade deals	Drive past			
	Deferred maintenance	X	X							
Very motivated (Vendor has little or no time)	Financial distress	X	X	X	X	X		Business forces sale, quick sale	**Price**	Quick settlement, cash offer
	Divorce	X	X	X	X	X		Mortgagee sale, desperate, keen		Remove their stress
Can't keep the property	Management difficulties	X	X		X	X		Deceased estate, urgent sale, beat the bank		
	Urgent maintenance	X	X		X		X	Must sell, all offers considered		
Must have the cash	Bad health	X	X	X				Vendor gives up, handyman needed		
	Retired & needing cash	X	X	X	X			Builder walks away		
	Business commitments	X	X	X	X	X		Unfinished		
	Death	X	X	X	X	X				

on the price or the terms and which negotiation tactics
to use.

▶ **Whether you should focus on terms or price** – It is commonly
understood in the real estate industry that a purchaser can
generally choose either the terms or the price when they
are buying a property. Someone who is desperate to sell will
typically dictate the terms (i.e. 'I need the cash next week')
but has little say over what price they will accept. In contrast,
someone who is not desperate but still wants to sell is more
likely to be in a position to dictate the price and let the buyer
choose the terms.

Step Two: Create equity

Once you have adequate cash you will need to focus on creating
some equity from your next property purchase . . . so buy a
property in a hot spot where the equity will be created by market
momentum. Depending on how much effort you want to put
in, you may also choose to buy a property that you can add
significant value to (and then add the value to it as soon as you
buy it). Of course, your safest option is to both buy a property in a
hot spot *and* then to add value to it before reselling. Doing both is
essential, in my opinion, for your first few property purchases at
least, especially if you have borrowed the entire purchase price,
because adding value wisely can reduce your risk.

Adding Value

When you consider adding value to any property you should
attempt to achieve the best improvement in value for the least cost
or what I refer to as getting more 'bang per buck'.

Below is a brief list of just a few potential improvements and
their respective bang per buck. As you can see, my number one

improvement for increasing a property's value, in relation to the cost of doing so, is paint!

Look for inexpensive ways to cosmetically improve your property.

IMPROVEMENT TO PROPERTY	BANG PER BUCK
Paint	Excellent
Renovate kitchens and bathrooms	Excellent
Replace front door	Excellent
Lift carpets and polish floor	Excellent
Reconfigure (i.e. add another bedroom)	Excellent
Replace wall coverings (or paint them)	Excellent
Replace worn carpet with good second-hand carpet	Very Good
Replace light fittings	Very Good
Remove unsightly add-ons	Very Good
Improve kerb appeal	Very Good
Add paving, terraces, decks	Good
Add a well-planted garden	Good
Fix everything that's broken	Good
Replace light switches, door handles	Good
Tidy yard and landscape	Good

The more of these improvements you combine, the better the ultimate look and feel the property has, therefore giving you the ability to maximise your return when you sell it. This list is not comprehensive – there are plenty of books dedicated entirely to the topic of adding value to real estate.

Step Three: Decide whether to sell or retain the property

You will need to measure the actual capital growth rate that your property experiences while you own it in order to manage your way to achieving your goal. Make sure you do not rely on misleading or flawed data (see Chapter 2).

If your expected capital growth does not eventuate then you will need to assess whether to hold the property for a longer time, bearing in mind the impact time has on risk (see Chapter 1).

Once you reach your capital growth goal then you need to seriously consider whether to prepare the property for sale and take your profit, or to retain ownership of it. If the hot spot drivers indicate further strong capital growth rates for the location then you have the option of retaining it in the short term. If you do choose to retain ownership you must continue to closely monitor ongoing capital growth rates to ensure they are adequate to achieve your goal.

If you decide to sell the property make sure any delayed maintenance is attended to because you need to present the property at its best to get the best sale price. Always present your properties for sale in pristine condition.

Then go back to Step One.

Chapter Summary

▶ Investing in hot spots without a clear goal will most likely result in confusion when you are making buying and selling decisions.

▶ Research the hot spot drivers for locations to identify individual hot spots.

▶ Consult professional advisors.

▶ To capitalise on a real estate hot spot you will need adequate cash or equity. Usually you need at least 10 per cent of the purchase price as a deposit – a financial institution can lend you the balance.

▶ If you have no available cash, you should convert your resources into either enough cash *or* enough cash flow so you can raise a deposit.

▶ Highly motivated vendors are often the most willing to negotiate.

▶ When adding value to any property you should attempt to achieve the best improvement in value for the least cost.

7

CHAPTER

Fear and Greed

- ▶ Fear, greed and hot spots
- ▶ Common manifestations of fear
- ▶ Common manifestations of greed

Fear, greed and hot spots

The potential consequences of acting out of fear or greed can be devastating, both financially and emotionally. Fear and greed are the two major motivating emotions which cause you to take action even when you don't want to. Be aware of this and always ask yourself, 'What is motivating me to take action in this situation?' If fear or greed are found to be your prime motivators then you had better take a much closer look at the facts before you take action. It can be difficult to recognise fear and greed before the event so consider your motivations carefully.

When investing in real estate hot spots you must *always* be prepared to walk away from every potential opportunity. There will always be another hot spot emerging somewhere, so don't let yourself be put under any time pressure to act until you have at least done your hot spots homework on the location first. If you have only just started your research when you find a bargain, which you fear you will miss out on if you don't buy it right now, I still say don't buy it until you have completed your research of the location and you know it is a hot spot!

Common manifestations of fear

Fear manifests in many different ways in real estate hot spots. Fear is typically an emotion with a high price attached, a high potential return, or both, and it can be responsible for ultimately decimating the value of a suburb or at least resulting in little, no, or negative capital growth for many years. People act on fear because of the potential harmful consequences of not acting on it.

To illustrate the emotion of fear, imagine this: You are standing atop a multi-storey building and across the street from you is another multi-storey building with a plank of wood running between the two. Someone is standing on the building across the road holding a $100 bill over the edge. They yell out to you that you can have the $100 if you cross the plank within the next five minutes or they will drop the $100 off the edge of the building. The motivating emotion in this case is greed, but I am sure you are not greedy enough to risk your life, walking across the plank for $100. In contrast, now imagine that instead of holding a $100 bill they are holding your life partner out over the edge of the building and you can only have them back if you cross the plank within the next five minutes or they will drop them off the edge of the building. Now the motivating emotion is fear and I am sure that if you were put in a fearful situation such as this that you would risk your life for your life partner.

That's an extreme example of the motivational impact of fear. However, it illustrates the point that fear can lead you to do things you would otherwise never do.

Acting on fear is cemented by time pressure. Because of this time pressure the potential consequences of acting on fear are sometimes not adequately considered before taking action.

Here are some likely manifestations of fear in real estate hot spots and why such manifestations become an option that some will choose to accept.

Fear of loss

The fear of loss can motivate you to make real estate purchasing decisions before you have thoroughly considered the level of risk involved. This fear is dangerous because it manifests in the form of feeling you must buy right now or you will miss out on any capital growth. This fear of loss is cemented because it instils a time pressure to act immediately.

The fear of loss also manifests when you are motivated *not* to buy real estate, for example, when there is the fear of a real estate crash. Of course, the fear of loss can be a healthy one, but only when the fear is a result of known facts rather than just opinion. If you act on *unsubstantiated* opinion, the lost opportunity cost can be significant. I have seen many real estate investors become 'frozen' when this occurred, even though there were clearly no genuine signals that a crash may occur. Ironically, this provided a perfect opportunity for those who were well-informed to capitalise on hot spots with less competition as fewer buyers were apparent in the market.

Another form of the fear of loss is the occurrence of unforeseen 'one off' events (such as tsunamis, earthquakes, terrorism, epidemics, etc), which can significantly impact on real estate values. If you fear you may suffer a loss as a result of those types of events then you may never invest in any real estate. There is no way I am aware of to minimise risks against such events, apart from not having all your wealth in real estate – but even then other investment returns may also suffer detrimentally from such events.

Consequences

The fear of loss which motivates you to buy *now* can lead you to becoming financially overcommitted, if you choose to borrow to a level that you can not comfortably afford. In extreme cases this could result in a forced sale by a financier and result in effectively wiping out all equity you may have in the property or even leading to your bankruptcy.

The fear of loss which motivates you *not* to buy *now* can result in significant missed opportunity cost.

Fear of unaffordability

The fear of unaffordability can motivate some to make premature real estate purchasing decisions. This fear is the belief that real estate in a location will continue to increase in value so significantly that it will become too expensive for you to purchase any real estate there. This belief is cemented because it instils a time pressure. The thought that you will never be able to afford to buy in this location unless you buy now puts a lot of pressure on you to act quickly.

Consequences

The fear of unaffordability can, ironically, lead you to become financially overcommitted by stretching your finances to a level you can not comfortably afford. In extreme cases this could result in a forced sale by a financier and, effectively, in wiping out all equity you may have in the property or even leading to your bankruptcy.

Common manifestations of greed

Greed doesn't need the same level of commitment for people to act that fear often brings. People act on greed because of the pleasure they will derive from it in contrast to people acting on fear because of the harm of the potential consequences from not acting on it.

Some of the manifestations of greed can be so subtle that it can be hard to distinguish whether you are being motivated by greed or you simply want a good return from investing.

Here are some likely manifestations of greed in real estate hot spots and why such manifestations become an option that some will choose to accept.

You believe you are on a winning streak so you can't lose

If every time you have invested in real estate in the past you have made a financial gain or won and you now believe you can't lose, then think again. Don't fool yourself into believing that just because you haven't suffered a loss so far from real estate investment that you won't make a loss at some time in the future. If you have a cavalier attitude to investing in real estate, you can lose money relatively easily. I am only too conscious of this, which is why I am so keen to minimise my risks with thorough research.

Consequences

Sooner or later the greed of the winning streak will lead to some investors becoming financially overcommitted. Sometimes their cash flow becomes crippled by non-performing real estate in a falling market, resulting in the inability to sell the real estate to recover all funds owed to the financiers. In extreme cases this could result in a forced sale by a financier and, effectively, in wiping out all equity you may have in the property or even leading to your bankruptcy.

You believe real estate is very safe so you can't lose

There is *always* the potential for real estate values to fall. So while most of us *intend* to invest safely, our definition of investing safely depends upon our perspective. What one person perceives as safe or low risk, another person may perceive as an unacceptable level of risk. Real estate has typically proven to be a relatively low-risk investment over the long term; however, many real estate investors commence their investing with a cavalier attitude of just buying any property because it will increase in value and is a low-risk investment. To have that attitude to real estate investing may be exciting but may end up proving costly. It is important to bear in mind that it *is* possible to lose money through real estate investing – never believe that you can't lose because real estate is a safe investment.

Consequences

The belief that real estate is always safe can eventually lead to the same consequences as the winning-streak attitude. While it is generally true that in the long term real estate values always increase, sometimes the time it takes before values actually do rise significantly diminishes your return.

History is littered with examples of house prices declining over the long term, but eventually they will increase again and tend to prove inflation-proof – eventually, but sometimes not for a decade or longer, like has occurred in Germany and Japan. Other times huge wealth is created as a result of capital growth which can make you feel invincible. A portion of this wealth is often borrowed against the increased real estate values to fund the purchase of more real estate and there is nothing in itself wrong with that.

But this can potentially lead to what I call 'reinvestment folly'. Don't get me wrong, I'm not against reinvesting in more real estate by using the equity you already have in owned real estate, but when such reinvestment is not accompanied by a thorough knowledge and understanding of the real estate cycle and real estate hot spots then I call it reinvestment folly.

For some this reinvestment folly offers an exciting 'living on the edge' dimension to their lives but for others it proves a costly exercise. When the market 'goes bad' and values do decline, it is extremely costly in many ways and can easily wipe out financial wealth in just a few months – not to mention the countless broken relationships resulting from financial pressure. People suffering from reinvestment folly often only recognise their investing mistakes when they are forced to sell down their property portfolio. That's an expensive way to learn the lesson of reinvestment folly.

Speculation without thorough research, knowledge and understanding of the real estate cycle and real estate hot spots adds an extra but unnecessary dimension of risk to real estate investing.

AN INSIDER'S GUIDE TO REAL ESTATE HOT SPOTS

Fear and Greed Secrets

Don't let fear or greed motivate your actions.

Always be prepared to walk away from every opportunity.

Don't lose touch with the market or with reality!

Learn to balance your acceptable level of risk with your expected level of return.

Chapter Summary

- The potential consequences of acting out of fear or greed can be devastating, both financially and emotionally.
- Fear manifests in many different ways in real estate hot spots. Fear is typically an emotion with a high price attached, a high potential return, or both, and it can be responsible for ultimately decimating the value of a suburb or at least resulting in little, no, or negative capital growth for many years.
- Fear can be costly in terms of lost capital or lost opportunity.
- The manifestation of greed can be very subtle and you may be unable to distinguish it from simply wanting a good return on your investment.
- Greed can lead to financial demise.
- Speculation without thorough research, knowledge and understanding of the real estate cycle and real estate hot spots adds an extra and unnecessary dimension of risk to real estate investing.

8

The Real Estate Cycle and Hot Spots

- ❭ The real estate cycle
- ❭ The three phases of the real estate cycle
- ❭ What is the real estate cycle clock?
- ❭ Where in the world does the real estate cycle exist?
- ❭ The real estate cycle in action

The real estate cycle

In my book *Grow Rich with the Property Cycle*, I explain at length the workings and influence of the real estate cycle on real estate markets. The real estate cycle is extremely relevant to the concept of real estate hot spots so this chapter introduces the concept of the real estate cycle.

When I first began studying and analysing the concept of a real estate cycle I almost did not want to believe that it may exist or, if it did, that it may be quite predictable. I thought that if a real estate cycle actually existed and it could be predicted then surely more people would have already used it to their financial advantage and the secret would already be out! To my pleasant surprise I found enough evidence to conclude that the real estate cycle clearly does exist. It has some immutable aspects, is measurable and also is quite predictable. I also gained some insight into why more people do not use it to their advantage.

Definition of the real estate cycle

An irregular but recurrent and predictable succession of causes and effects that the real estate market experiences with resultant impacts on the creation and destruction of real estate wealth.

Understanding the real estate cycle lies in the fact that the cycle is exactly what its name suggests . . . a cycle of recurring events. However, I have also discovered that many intelligent investors have failed to use the real estate cycle to their advantage. This appears to be due to the powerful emotions of fear and greed that are evident throughout the real estate cycle. The majority of real estate investors tend to react emotionally without even realising it.

There is every indication that the same real estate cycle exists in any country's residential real estate market where supply and demand are driven by a free market combined with a deregulated finance industry without significant intervention from political or government forces. If the finance industry is either underdeveloped or overly protected by regulation, then imbalance or volatility can interfere with the traditional real estate cycle progress. Historically when countries have deregulated their finance industry at the same time as having favourable tax law for real estate investment, a real estate price bubble has occurred and resulted in a subsequent significant correction in real estate values.

The three phases of the real estate cycle

There is much confusion about the real estate cycle, often caused by sensational media headlines combined with many differing opinions on whether real estate is a sound investment vehicle or not.

The real estate cycle has sometimes been interpreted as including several phases, ranging from a real estate bust to a real estate boom. However, when you look at the historical performance of the real estate market, it becomes clear that the real estate cycle only consists of three major phases.

The real estate cycle consistently and repetitively experiences these three distinct phases during each complete cycle. I have labelled these three phases *boom*, *slump* and *recovery*.

What is the real estate cycle clock?

The real estate cycle follows a consistent pattern. To help gauge the progress of the real estate cycle I have invented the real estate cycle clock – a simple device that real estate investors can use to follow the progress of the real estate cycle.

Each phase of the real estate cycle is reflected by the state of the real estate market at the time. For example, in the boom phase real estate is an extremely popular investment vehicle and highly sought after. The real estate market is in a state of euphoria as real estate investors and homeowners experience strong capital growth in the value of their real estate. However, in the slump, and for most of the recovery phase, real estate is typically out of favour and therefore the state of the real estate market is somewhat subdued. Real estate is not experiencing strong growth in value and may even be experiencing a decline in value.

As mentioned earlier in this book real estate hot spots tend to be more prevalent during the recovery and boom phases as this is typically when cyclical hot spots emerge. However, hot spots *can* and *do* emerge during the slump, providing enough hot spot drivers are increasing demand beyond the level of supply within a specific location as discussed in Chapter 3.

The easiest way to understand the progress of the real estate cycle is to represent its phases by the circular shape of a typical clock.

The illustration opposite shows the three real estate cycle phases in the format of a clock. This real estate cycle clock follows a clockwise movement from one phase to the next. However, unlike a normal clock, the length of each phase can vary from one real estate cycle to the next. Likewise, the duration of one phase will not necessarily determine the duration of the following phases.

Where in the world does the real estate cycle exist?

Whether you are investing in New Zealand, the UK, Ireland, Australia, the USA, Sweden, Norway, Finland or even parts of Asia, the same basic real estate cycle can be seen historically. These simple patterns have become particularly evident since the mid-1980s when financial deregulation occurred in many of these countries. The real estate cycle can often become exaggerated and prolonged by larger populations causing sustained rises or declines in either the supply of real estate or the demand for real estate.

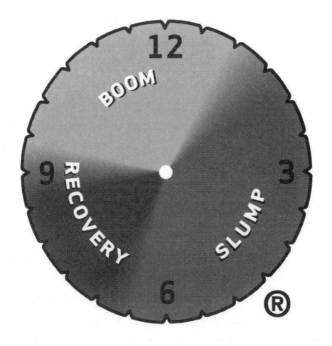

The real estate cycle clock

This appears to be a result of the greater momentum created by larger populations.

Irrespective of a population's size, the real estate cycle can be volatile. This volatility can result in real estate values oscillating significantly. There have been periods when real estate values have decreased so far that a significant portion of the population has had negative equity in their real estate portfolio (i.e. when the owner owes more than the real estate is currently worth). This situation occurred in the early 1990s in New Zealand and the UK.

The same dynamics and principles that have ruled the New Zealand real estate cycle since financial deregulation occurred in the mid-1980s apply to every free market-dominated country in the world. There are some country-specific influencers on real estate markets throughout the world (for example, the treatment of tax issues such as depreciation and capital gains) which can exaggerate the effects on real estate values, but the real estate cycle follows the same basic progression regardless of these influencers.

The New Zealand real estate cycle offers an excellent model to study as New Zealand has a largely deregulated real estate and finance industry. This means that the free market reigns in respect of real estate values and consequently the real estate cycle operates efficiently from an economic perspective. New Zealand is also a relatively small economy so its real estate cycles tend to be shorter than those of larger economies.

This makes the study of the causes and effects of the various forces driving the real estate cycle relatively easy to identify.

While the concept of the real estate cycle is not a recent discovery, little research on real estate cycles had been undertaken internationally prior to 1980. Today there is widespread acknowledgement that real estate cycles exist and much debate over whether future real estate cycles can be predicted. My research, outlined in *Grow Rich with the Property Cycle*, indicates that real estate cycles are predictable as they follow a basic pattern. This pattern was discovered over seventy years ago by the grandfather of the real estate cycle concept, an American by the name of Homer Hoyt. In his book *100 Years of Land Values in Chicago*, written in 1933, he analyses the movement of Chicago's land values and notes that a recurrent succession of causes and effects impacted on these values during the hundred years from 1830 to 1930. Hoyt concluded that a real estate cycle certainly existed and identified some of its consistent key drivers. Hoyt noted that key drivers such as population growth often created initial increased demand for real estate. This increased demand was followed by a sharp rise in rents which resulted in increased land values because of the greater financial returns available from buildings. Hoyt then observed the subsequent and inevitable oversupply of real estate caused by a significant increase in construction of new buildings as a result of higher margins being achieved by construction firms. Finally, too much new construction produced an oversupply of real estate that eventually resulted in rent reductions and subsequent real estate price erosion. This pattern still appears in real estate markets today and is possibly even more apparent due to the ready availability and quality of current statistical data.

The more you invest in residential real estate, the more critical it becomes to understand the real estate cycle. It surprises me that even experienced investors sometimes get caught out by the real estate cycle and end up losing much, if not all, of their real estate wealth. History is littered with examples of formerly successful real estate investors who have suffered huge losses as a result of not paying attention to the real estate cycle and by falling victim to their own fear or greed.

The real estate cycle in action

The real estate cycle is predictable but it is not an exact science. Some people believe history never repeats but I am not convinced that is so. I believe historic real estate cycles can give us some insight into what may be in store in the future.

The following graphs reveal the distinct pattern of the real estate cycle in several different countries from the mid to late 1980s and throughout the 1990s. They reveal varying degrees of real estate price growth, but the three distinct stages of the real estate cycle can be seen in each country. (Of course there are local real estate cycles within the major cities, regions and centres of each country, but for the purpose of this overview I have considered the real estate cycle of each of these countries as a whole.)

The following graphs indicate the real estate cycles of each country in action from the mid-1980s.

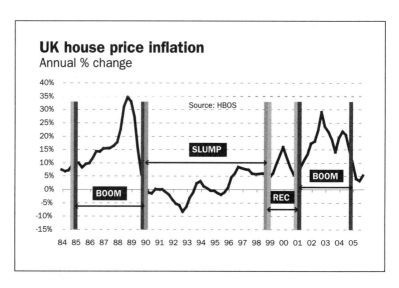

Graph 8.1

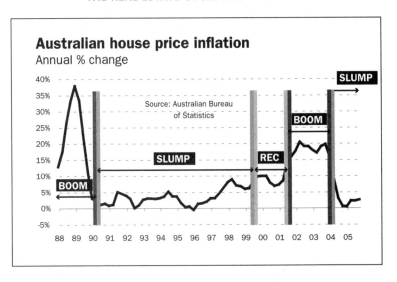

Graph 8.2

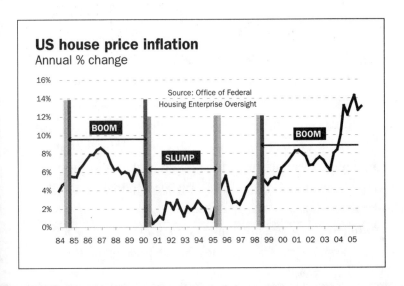

Graph 8.3

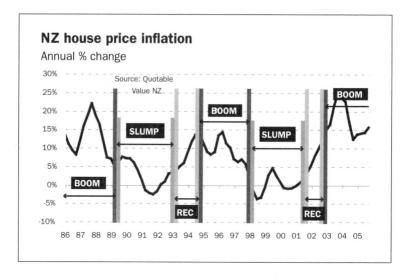

Graph 8.4

You will observe that the most extreme house price growth is recorded in the UK (Graph 8.1) and Australia (Graph 8.2) during the late 1980s when house price inflation peaked in those countries at around 35 per cent per annum. Both of these countries then experienced a long slump phase.

In contrast, the USA and New Zealand experienced lower house price growth at their peaks in the late 1980s, with the USA being much lower, followed by a much shorter duration of the slump phase in both of these countries compared to the UK and Australia.

While the data are not sufficient to draw a strong conclusion from, it appears that very strong house price growth may well result in an extended slump phase.

The duration of a complete real estate cycle has not proved consistent, and has typically lasted for anything from seven to eighteen years. The longevity of each real estate cycle obviously varies depending on the state of the key drivers for each country. It also appears that a smaller economy such as New Zealand's can experience faster cycles, and this may well be attributable to the increased volatility and limited inertia of the key drivers of the real estate cycle in smaller economies.

It is interesting to consider the time lapse between the peak of each boom and the peak of each slump so I have graphed these below.

Some useful observations are the long durations between the peak of one boom to that of the next boom and the durations between the troughs of one slump and the next slump. But the most interesting observation of all must be the relatively short duration between the peak of a boom and the trough of a slump which follows.

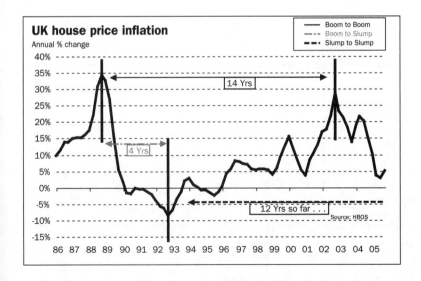

Graph 8.5

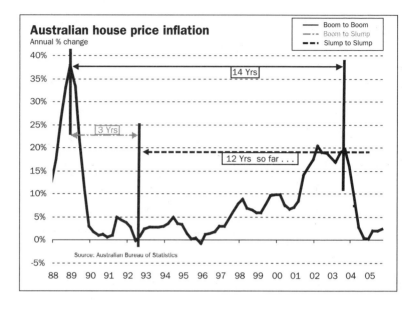

Graph 8.6

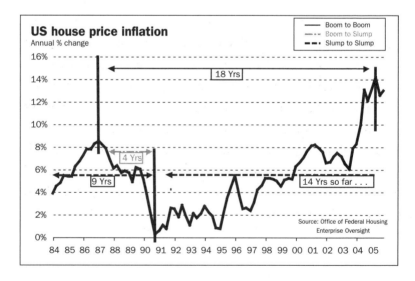

Graph 8.7

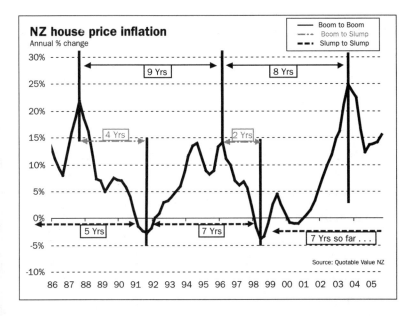

Graph 8.8

I have considered whether the duration in time of any specific phase has any consistent influence on the duration of a subsequent phase, but have found no clear evidence that this is the case. Certainly, over the last decade New Zealand's real estate cycles have been significantly shorter than those in larger economies such as the UK, USA and Australia. I have no hard evidence but I suspect this has to do with New Zealand's nimble economy which reacts quickly to a combination of changes in the key drivers of the real estate cycle compared with the bigger economies which have a much greater momentum.

Chapter Summary

▸ The real estate cycle is a cycle of recurring events.

▸ There are three distinct phases during each cycle: boom, slump and recovery.

▸ Hot spots tend be more prevalent during the recovery and boom phases, however they can and do occur during the slump phase.

▸ The duration of a complete real estate cycle has not proved consistent and has typically lasted for anything from seven to eighteen years. The longevity of each real estate cycle obviously varies depending on the state of the key drivers for each country.

▸ The duration of any specific real estate cycle phase has not proven to have any consistent influence on the duration of a subsequent phase.

9

A Country Perspective on Hot Spots and Real Estate Crashes

- ▶ A 'big picture' country perspective – USA case study
- ▶ Can hot spots emerge during a real estate crash?
- ▶ Are we heading for a real estate crash?
- ▶ What can cause a real estate crash?

A 'big picture' country perspective – USA case study

While I don't yet have access to the appropriate data to assess the potential of hot spots emerging in *every* major city, it is useful to consider the capital growth rates across each state in the USA to get a 'big picture' perspective of how much values have increased and why. This big picture country perspective is useful because it can give you some idea of which states the highest demand for real estate may be in. The states with the highest demand are likely to be demonstrating strong population growth and are also likely to contain hot spots.

The following images have been sourced from 'Bubble-proof your real estate investments' by Dolf de Roos and Andrew Waite with *Personal Real Estate Investor Magazine*.

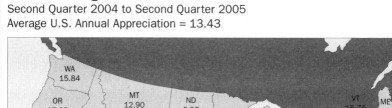

One Year Change in House Prices
Second Quarter 2004 to Second Quarter 2005
Average U.S. Annual Appreciation = 13.43

Graph 9.1

Looking at individual states we can see the capital growth rates range from the low of 4.68 per cent in Texas up to 28.13 per cent in Nevada. Other top performers include Arizona, California and Hawaii. To consider why these locations may have experienced such superior growth we need to assess what is driving the value increases. The first obvious driver to consider is population statistics because historically population surges have driven up

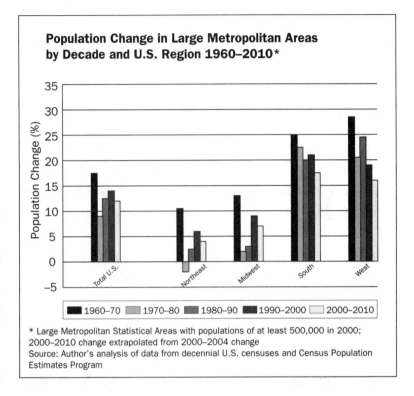

Population Change in Large Metropolitan Areas by Decade and U.S. Region 1960–2010*

* Large Metropolitan Statistical Areas with populations of at least 500,000 in 2000; 2000–2010 change extrapolated from 2000–2004 change
Source: Author's analysis of data from decennial U.S. censuses and Census Population Estimates Program

Graph 9.2

real estate values. The larger the population increase the higher the demand for real estate to rent or buy.

So if we consider the population changes for each region and identify those with the strongest population increases, we get some idea of which areas are likely to have stronger than average rates of growth.

Some cities and suburbs within cities will have experienced even higher capital growth rates than seen in their state. Often this is attributable to those locations receiving a comparatively high percentage of the state's overall population increase.

Population growth in itself is great for creating demand and as we can see from the data above, the south and west of the USA had the strongest population growth and the strongest capital growth rates. However, these locations have also demonstrated many other hot spot drivers such as aggressive urban renewal, including substantial new amenities, new and improved access and transport links, new and improved schooling, and shortage of available properties to meet demand. Of course, some of these locations will cease to be hot spots at some point in time. Although the above data bodes well for the USA's south and west real estate values, it is still critical to consider the status of all the hot spot drivers for these locations as they can quickly change and subsequently quickly cease to be hot spots. For example, if there are too many properties being built and available for sale then the market can become oversupplied and values may fall even in light of strong population growth.

Can hot spots emerge during a real estate crash?

While it is comforting to be able to assess hot spot drivers to identify hot spots there is always the concern that the slump phase of the real estate cycle may actually deliver a real estate crash. This can detrimentally affect real estate values in every location within a country. The likelihood of hot spots emerging during a real estate crash is low because all real estate tends to be affected by a real estate crash. Any hot spots that do emerge are likely to have a very limited time as a hot spot because confidence in property is likely to be very low, and economic and real estate market drivers are likely to be absent.

The potential for former hot spots to become cold spots increases in the event of a real estate crash. This is because the suburbs surrounding the hot spot will experience a decrease in values. So for values to remain at the existing levels in the hot spot the premium that people are prepared to pay for real estate there must increase. Of course, a real estate crash also affects the local economy, delivering an economic impact which again is likely to put a quick stop to any hot spots. When the local economy suffers, fewer people can afford the luxury of living in the latest hot spot and, therefore, demand reduces, most likely causing values to fall.

Are we heading for a real estate crash?

The Economist has been tracking house price growth rates for several years and recently produced the following graph, which reveals the longevity and magnitude of house price growth rates since 1998.

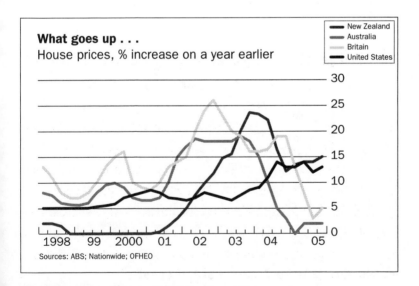

Graph 9.3 *The Economist*, 16 June 2005

In the graph below we can see that since 2000 the USA and New Zealand have not had the cumulative growth that the UK and Australia have seen. This data indicates that out of these four economies, in 2006, the UK market is probably the most overheated in this cycle with Australia next and then the USA and New Zealand. So the USA and New Zealand's cyclical slump following the recent boom may be relatively soft compared to the UK and Australia's cyclical slump which could be harder or more protracted. 'The higher they rise the harder they fall' is most likely an appropriate statement in this regard.

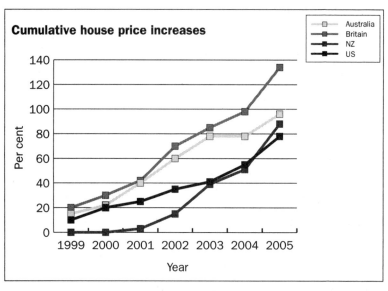

Graph 9.4 The same data expressed as cumulative numbers.

What can cause a real estate crash?

There are plenty of books dedicated to the topic of real estate crashes so I have outlined below a summary of my limited research into historic real estate crashes. I made some interesting observations which dispel some myths; like the myth that every cycle ends in a crash.

Before we consider the concept of a crash we need to define what constitutes a boom and a bust. The Federal Deposit Insurance Corp (FDIC) has defined both as follows:

A boom is an increase in values of 30 per cent* or more in three years.

A bust is a decrease in values of −15 per cent* or more in five years.

(* The percentage is inflation-adjusted, i.e. value changes after inflation is deducted)

During the slump phase of the property cycle only about 20 per cent of recorded real estate booms in the USA have resulted in a bust. So it would seem not every boom is followed by a bust.

While only 20 per cent of booms result in busts the other 80 per cent all suffered from what can only be described as stagnation. They still enjoyed price rises of about 2 per cent per annum (inflation-adjusted) in the following five years.

Major reasons cited historically for busts in housing values in the USA have been:

▶ Strong negative net migration
▶ Localised economic stress or recession
▶ Commercial real estate collapse. This quickly flows into downward pressure on housing values.
▶ Oil price shocks. Oil price rises are considered bad for economic growth (crippling the economy) and provide 'fuel' for inflation. High inflation does not automatically translate into higher property prices, but quickly increases property ownership costs (i.e. rates, insurance, repairs and maintenance, etc). The flow-on effects of oil price rises are expected to be felt throughout the entire economy as the

higher cost of transporting goods will be passed back to consumers in the form of higher prices for goods and services resulting in higher inflation. At the level of US$70/barrel the world economy becomes seriously threatened . . .

(Source: BT Funds Management Ltd)

It is worth noting that every recession in the USA in the last 35 years was preceded by a sharp run-up in oil prices.

Of course, the fact that oil price shocks can lead to a real estate bust is a cause for major concern at the time of writing this book in 2006. Volatile oil supplies have seen a sharp run-up in oil prices of more than 50 per cent in 2005/06.

Unfortunately many countries' governing banks will probably feel the need to increase interest rates to attempt to counter increasing inflation, and this will only force real estate markets into a harder landing than they would otherwise have had.

Chapter Summary

▶ The 'big picture' country perspective in this example is useful for observing which US states the highest demand for real estate may be in. The states with the highest demand are likely to have strong population growth and to contain hot spots within them while they are experiencing strong population growth.

▶ The first obvious driver to consider is population statistics because historically population surges have driven up real estate values. The larger the population increase the higher the demand for real estate to rent or buy.

▶ Cities and suburbs within cities may experience higher capital growth rates than seen in their state because they have a comparatively high percentage of the state's overall population increase.

▶ The likelihood of hot spots emerging during a real estate crash is low.

▶ Major reasons cited for busts in housing values historically in the USA have been strong negative net migration, localised economic stress, oil price shocks, and commercial real estate collapse.

▶ Every recession in the USA in the last 35 years was preceded by a sharp run-up in oil prices.

Tables of SuburbWatch Movements for Cyclical Hot Spots

The data measures the single quarter capital growth rate as **Qtr** and then the rolling annual growth rate as **Ann**.

The locations are all suburbs within the same city of Auckland, New Zealand. Suburb names have been removed as this data is privately owned and unable to be freely redistributed in terms of the supply agreement for this data. The patterns that emerge are more important than the actual locations' names.

Notes:
- The underlined numbers in the Qtr columns represent either the first quarter where more than 4 per cent growth was achieved or the two consecutive quarters where more than 8 per cent growth was achieved.
- The numbers in italics represent the annual growth rate that was achieved if you bought real estate within the location in the quarter immediately *after* using the more than 4 per cent

in one quarter or the more than 8 per cent in two quarters as a buy signal. (WARNING: This is typically not a buy signal if the real estate cycle is in the mid to late boom phase or the slump phase!)

▶ Note that every location except location G revealed a more than 8 per cent growth rate in two quarters to the first quarter of 2002, but location G did reveal a more than 4 per cent growth rate in the same first quarter of 2002.

▶ Note the cyclical influence delivering a strong quarter for all of these locations in the third quarter of 2003 and that quarter's growth spurt was the effect of the real estate cycle being in full boom benefiting every one of these locations.

In the event a location experiences either of these rates of growth (more than 4 per cent in 1 Qtr or more than 8 per cent in 2 Qtrs) *and* the location is experiencing the real estate cycle recovery or early- to mid-boom phase, then the location is likely to remain or become a cyclical hot spot for the next six to twelve months or more.

The locations again reveal the buy signals based purely on their capital growth rates (in the fourth quarter of 2003 or the first quarter of 2004) but then deliver low annual capital growth rates in the following year in locations B, C, D, F, G and H.

This is because in late 2003 Auckland was already past the mid-boom phase of the real estate cycle.

LOCATION	A		B		C		D		E		F		G		H	
Date	Ann	Qtr	Ann	Qtr	Ann	Qtr	Ann	Qtr	Ann	Qtr	Ann	Qtr	Ann	Qtr	Ann	Qtr
2000Q1	7.5	1.1	11.0	2.6	4.4	0.2	7.4	2.1	-1.8	-2.0	1.3	-1.9	-2.1	-1.7	-0.3	-1.6
2000Q2	3.8	0.1	6.1	0.9	1.0	-1.2	9.0	0.6	-10.9	-3.6	-1.7	1.4	-6.6	-0.4	-1.4	1.9
2000Q3	6.0	-1.6	13.8	1.9	3.7	0.5	8.1	0.1	-1.8	3.6	2.4	-0.3	-4.8	-2.3	-1.5	-3.1
2000Q4	2.4	2.8	3.4	-2.0	1.0	1.5	1.0	-1.8	-3.3	-1.3	-1.2	-0.4	-4.4	0.0	0.1	2.9
2001Q1	2.8	1.5	1.5	0.7	1.9	1.1	1.1	2.2	-2.4	-1.1	2.9	2.2	-0.3	2.4	3.7	2.0
2001Q2	4.4	1.7	-0.1	-0.7	3.1	0.0	1.7	1.2	1.3	0.1	0.4	-1.1	1.2	1.1	1.7	-0.1
2001Q3	6.4	0.4	1.9	3.9	3.7	1.1	4.6	3.0	0.6	2.9	2.6	1.9	4.0	0.5	6.6	1.8
2001Q4	5.3	1.7	5.6	1.7	4.2	2.0	8.4	2.0	3.2	1.3	6.1	3.1	7.2	3.2	7.3	3.6
2002Q1	11.2	7.4	12.2	7.3	10.7	7.6	13.6	7.4	13.8	9.5	9.5	5.6	9.1	4.3	13.7	8.4
2002Q2	14.6	5.1	18.8	5.9	14.5	3.8	16.9	4.5	15.2	1.5	15.1	4.5	11.0	3.0	18.1	4.3
2002Q3	20.3	6.1	16.9	2.0	20.1	6.7	18.7	4.8	18.3	6.0	19.5	6.3	16.8	6.3	21.8	5.5
2002Q4	29.8	11.2	19.9	4.7	21.1	3.0	20.5	3.8	21.2	4.2	21.0	4.6	18.5	4.9	24.0	5.8
2003Q1	27.1	4.7	16.9	4.3	19.5	6.0	20.2	7.1	17.5	5.8	24.0	8.6	17.2	3.0	20.3	4.7
2003Q2	24.6	2.6	10.4	-0.6	16.7	1.0	16.9	1.2	18.8	2.8	21.4	1.9	17.8	3.6	20.8	4.8
Cyclical Influence																
2003Q3	29.0	10.5	15.4	7.0	17.7	7.7	19.8	7.7	23.8	11.0	25.6	10.5	23.0	11.5	20.0	4.7
2003Q4	21.6	3.8	15.0	4.3	23.0	8.3	17.2	1.2	23.3	3.7	25.1	4.1	25.5	7.4	22.5	8.3
2004Q1	15.3	-1.6	10.5	-0.2	12.5	-4.5	16.6	6.5	21.3	3.8	20.1	3.6	23.2	0.7	16.6	-1.2
2004Q2	16.7	4.0	12.7	1.6	15.2	3.7	16.6	1.2	19.4	0.9	14.8	-3.4	19.3	-0.3	13.3	1.5
2004Q3	12.8	6.6	-1.1	-6.8	14.3	6.8	14.1	5.2	11.7	3.3	7.2	2.9	8.8	1.0	9.3	0.7
2004Q4	0.4	-8.6	-4.6	0.8	3.0	-3.0	10.2	-2.7	5.4	-2.6	4.4	1.3	1.7	0.3	-1.0	-2.0
2005Q1	10.1	8.1	1.2	5.6	12.6	5.1	5.8	2.1	2.1	0.5	-0.1	-0.9	3.4	2.4	5.7	5.5
2005Q2	6.5	0.4	-1.9	-1.5	9.1	0.2	5.9	1.3	4.3	3.1	6.6	3.3	6.9	3.2	4.5	0.3
2005Q3	0.0	0.1	6.0	1.1	0.4	-1.9	2.7	2.0	3.4	2.4	5.2	1.5	8.2	2.3	9.2	5.4

187

ABOUT THE AUTHOR

Kieran Trass is a well-respected real estate author, real estate market analyst and regular commentator on the real estate cycle and the residential real estate market.

Kieran's history:
- Investment in residential real estate for twenty years.
- Finance industry experience in excess of twenty years, including working for local and international financial institutions both in New Zealand and overseas.
- Founding committee member of the Auckland Property Investors Association (APIA) in 1995.
- Secretary of the New Zealand Property Investors Federation in 1999.
- Regular media contributor on the topics of the real estate cycle and real estate markets.
- Regular guest speaker at real estate investment seminars including the New Zealand Property Investment Expo, New Zealand Property Investors Federation Annual Conferences, Real Estate Investor Associations throughout New Zealand, USA Chamber of Commerce, Sydney Investors Group, Millionaires in Training (Acumen Inc).

- ❱ Casual lecturer on real estate at both Massey University (Albany Campus) and Auckland University.
- ❱ Author of the book *Grow Rich with the Property Cycle*, Penguin Books, 2004.
- ❱ Real estate consultant and advisor to individuals and corporates.

More about the author's real estate cycle clock

The progress of the real estate cycle can give an incredibly powerful indication of what strategies real estate investors should be using and when to use them. The author has created a website dedicated to telling the time on the real estate cycle clock in various parts of the developed world. As the author's research of individual countries and their major cities' real estate cycles continues, these locations will be added to the Tell Me The Time website. To support the author's commitment to maintaining ongoing research into this specialised field this information is only available to paid subscribers.

Details can be found at **www.tellmethetime.com**

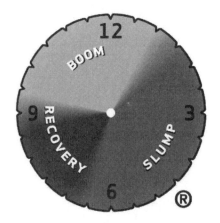

DISCLAIMER

Kieran Trass does not intend for the information contained in this book to be used as a substitute for personalised investment advice. Kieran Trass recommends that you seek the advice of financial, taxation and legal advisors before entering into any financial transaction or making any investment decision.

To the maximum extent permitted by law, Kieran Trass specifically excludes any liability for any error in or inaccuracy in, or omissions from, this book and disclaims any liability for any loss or damage which you or any other person may suffer by using or relying on any information in this book whether caused by negligence or otherwise.

Other titles by Kieran Trass

Grow Rich with the Property Cycle is Kieran Trass's first book.

Grow rich from residential property investment. Regardless of the property cycle phase – boom, slump or recovery – the trick is having the right knowledge and information.

Grow Rich with the Property Cycle will help you recognise the specific opportunities that the cycle provides to make more money from property investment.

Successful real estate investor, financier and advisor Kieran Trass shares the secrets learned from more than twenty years observing the property cycle in action.

Based on extensive research of property markets in New Zealand and major economies like Australia, the United States, and the United Kingdom. Whether you are a seasoned property investor or just starting out, this book will provide you with a clear understanding of the property cycle and how you can use it to grow rich.

GROW RICH

with the

PROPERTY CYCLE

Learn to predict booms and slumps
What smart investors know
What drives the PROPERTY CYCLE

KIERAN TRASS